teach® yourself

growing your own fruits and vegetables

michael thurlow

teach yourself 70 (1938 2008) celebrate with us

Launched in 1938, the **teach yourself** series grew rapidly in response to the world's wartime needs. Loved and trusted by over 50 million readers, the series has continued to respond to society's changing interests and passions and now, 70 years on, includes over 500 titles, from Arabic and Beekeepir What would you like to lear

be where you want to be w

For UK order enquiries: please contact Bookpoint Ltd, 130 Milton Park, Abingdon, Oxon OX14 4SB. Telephone: +44 (0) 1235 827720. Fax: +44 (0) 1235 400454. Lines are open 09.00–17.00, Monday to Saturday, with a 24-hour message answering service. Details about our titles and how to order are available at www.teachyourself.co.uk

For USA order enquiries: please contact McGraw-Hill Customer Services, PO Box 545, Blacklick, OH 43004-0545, USA. Telephone: 1-800-722-4726. Fax: 1-614-755-5645.

For Canada order enquiries: please contact McGraw-Hill Ryerson Ltd, 300 Water St, Whitby, Ontario L1N 9B6, Canada. Telephone: 905 430 5000. Fax: 905 430 5020.

Long renowned as the authoritative source for self-guided learning – with more than 50 million copies sold worldwide – the **teach yourself** series includes over 500 titles in the fields of languages, crafts, hobbies, business, computing and education.

British Library Cataloguing in Publication Data: a catalogue record for this title is available from the British Library.

Library of Congress Catalog Card Number: on file.

First published in UK 2009 by Hodder Education, part of Hachette UK, 338 Euston Road, London NW1 3BH.

First published in US 2009 by The McGraw-Hill Companies, Inc.

This edition published 2009.

The **teach yourself** name is a registered trade mark of Hodder Headline.

Copyright © 2009 Michael Thurlow

Typeset by Transet Limited, Coventry, England.
Printed in Great Britain for Hodder Education, an Hachette UK Company, 338 Euston Road, London NW1 3BH, by CPI Cox & Wyman, Reading, Berkshire RG1 8EX.

The publisher has used its best endeavours to ensure that the URLs for external websites referred to in this book are correct and active at the time of going to press. However, the publisher and the author have no responsibility for the websites and can make no guarantee that a site will remain live or that the content will remain relevant, decent or appropriate.

Hachette UK's policy is to use papers that are natural, renewable and recyclable products and made from wood grown in sustainable forests. The logging and manufacturing processes are expected to conform to the environmental regulations of the country of origin.

Impression number   10 9 8 7 6 5 4 3 2 1
Year   2013 2012 2011 2010 2009

contents

To Mary, my wife, for her unfailing support.

introduction

There was a time when fruit and vegetable growing had become the Cinderella of gardening. It had fallen out of favour as the shelves of the supermarkets bulged with mass-produced factory-farmed fruit and vegetables. The post-war housing boom saw millions of lawns, herbaceous borders and rose beds planted as gardeners created their own little paradise around them. Leisure gardening was here to stay, and why should you want to toil in the field growing food crops when everything that you could ever need was only a car drive away? There were brand new pesticides and herbicides being introduced at an alarming rate, which would take care of all of the 'nasties' in your garden. These were the golden days that would last forever. Sadly, all dreams have to come to an end when we wake up, and suddenly we were woken up with a start.

The chemicals that had once offered us the promise of a pest- and disease-free garden were now threatening to turn our planet into a sterile and lifeless desert as one species after another came under the threat of extinction from excessive chemical use. The voice of the cuckoo that for centuries had announced that summer was here was suddenly replaced with silence. This was an indication that things had changed and not necessarily for the better.

There is a growing concern among a large number of gardeners regarding what they consider to be the excessive use of pesticides and herbicides in the production of food crops. A classic example is the common apple, which can receive many applications of chemicals just to produce the perfect, blemish-free fruit. The support for the growing of fruit and vegetables without having to resort to the use of any form of chemicals is on the increase, and we hope to demonstrate to you through the pages of this book how to manage a fruit and vegetable garden successfully using modern organic techniques.

Growing and eating your own fruit and vegetables is one of the most satisfying experiences that you can ever enjoy. You do not have to be the owner of a large garden to achieve this dream; it is surprising just how productive even the smallest plot can be. It does not matter if you are the owner of a city courtyard garden or the smallest balcony, when containers such as raised beds, flowerpots and window boxes can all be used to provide fresh produce for the kitchen. Most modern houses do not have large gardens and what garden space there is around the house is just big enough to erect a rotary clothes line and park a car on.

You may have a young family and need space for them to play. If so, why not consider applying for an allotment garden? These provide a wonderful opportunity for all of the family to get their hands dirty and enjoy many happy hours outdoors together in the fresh air. What is more, you can eat and enjoy the results of your labours.

All it takes is a little imagination and a certain amount of perseverance to become an accomplished fruit and veggie grower. You won't regret it!

tools

Always choose the right tool for the job. When you first begin to garden it is quite easy to be overwhelmed by the vast range of designs that are available at garden centres and DIY outlets. Resist making any hasty decisions or impulse buys because you will only regret it later on. There are plenty of gardening tools for sale that really are poorly designed and manufactured. Do not be too proud or shy to seek the advice of other gardeners – ask if you can try out their spade or fork. You will be surprised to discover how different they will feel in your hands once you actually begin using them. Just bouncing tools up and down and tapping them on the floor of the store is not going to give you a good idea of how they will feel in practice. Also, as a result of a better standard of living since the end of the Second World War, people today are a lot taller than they used to be. This is acknowledged by the tool manufacturers, who are now producing spades and forks with longer shafts and handles. Most good outlets will carry a range of these tools for tall gardeners, although you may need to shop around to meet all of your requirements. Even the needs of junior gardeners are catered for. Several of the big-name tool companies produce a range of tools, from a spade to a wheelbarrow, that are specially designed for children.

Do not let the cost of buying new tools and equipment deter you from creating your vegetable plot. There are plenty of first-class spades, forks and so on available on the second-hand market. Some have hardly been used while others are well used, which can be an advantage in some cases. For example, when you first use a new spade it will feel heavy and a little clumsy, but after you have been digging with it for several months it will become lighter and easier to work with. This process is known as 'breaking in'; with used equipment the job has already been done for you by the previous owner. Always try to buy the best tools that you can afford – it is a false economy to purchase something just because it is in the sale. It may make you sound boring to your friends and family, but you could ask them to make a contribution towards your collection as a birthday or Christmas gift.

Top tip 🐛🌸

Always treat the wooden shafts and handles of all garden tools with linseed oil every month or so. As well as preserving the wood it reduces friction, allowing the wood to slide through your hands more easily, so preventing painful blisters and calluses forming. With brand new tools, remove the protective varnish using the blade of a gardener's knife, then rub the handle smooth with glass paper before applying the linseed oil with a rag.

What you will need

The following list describes the minimum range of gardening tools required to get you gardening. You do not have to purchase them all at once – to help spread the costs you can buy them as you need them. To keep them safe and in the best working order, they should always be stored somewhere dry and secure. Make it a habit to clean and oil your tools at the end of the working session. This will not only extend their life but will also make them safe and comfortable to use.

Courtyard, balcony garden, container/raised beds

Biscuit tin – to keep your seed packets in, safe from damage by moisture and vermin.

Ground sheet – this could be an old blanket or sheet of plastic, or it could be purpose made for the job. It will help to prevent creating a mess when re-potting or re-soiling beds/containers.

Hand fork – to cultivate the soil in the pots and containers.

Planting trowel – to make small planting holes for pot-grown plants.

Small table – not a necessity, but very handy to use as a potting bench or worktop.

Watering can – choose a small 5-litre (1-gallon) can. Watering raised beds and containers can be a time-consuming operation. You will become less tired if you are lifting smaller amounts of water. It may not be practical to use a hosepipe in a small or confined area. Also, the force of the jet of water could make a mess by scooping the compost/soil out of the containers.

Allotment/small vegetable plot

Biscuit tin – to keep your seed packets in, safe from damage by moisture and vermin.

Bucket/trug – convenient for carrying tools, fertilizers, compost, plants and harvested crops. Also very handy for filling with water to plunge dry plants in. The 'tub trug' is made from recycled tyres and is available in a variety of sizes and colours.

Digging fork – has four tines and is the same size as the spade. Used to dig the soil and to break it down into a more crumbly texture. It can also be used to lift potatoes and other root crops.

Digging spade – not to be confused with the smaller border spade. Used for all major digging and planting operations. The depth of a digging spade is always referred to as its 'spit'.

Garden line – this is used to plant or sow seeds in dead straight rows. It can be a manufactured article or homemade from two short sticks/rods and a length of garden string.

Garden rake – used to create a fine finish/tilth to the soil surface when preparing seedbeds.

Hoe – used to control weeds in the garden. There are several kinds of hoe; the most commonly used is the Dutch hoe. It slides through the top of the soil, severing the top of the weed from its root and leaving it to shrivel and die on the surface of the soil.

Planting trowel – used to create small planting holes for transplants or plants that have been grown in pots.

Watering can/hose (10 litre/2 gallon) – it is important to be able to water plants during the growing season. Using a watering can may seem very old fashioned but it does encourage you not to waste water. Dragging a hosepipe around the plot can damage plants; also, there is the temptation to spray water over the tops of the plants, leaving the ground underneath the foliage bone dry.

Wheelbarrow – a must for moving heavy or bulky items around the garden. Choose one with a pneumatic tyre as these are much easier to push and will not sink into soft ground.

> **Top tip**
> To make digging easier always sharpen the front of the blade of a spade using an engineer's file.

Top tip
Always store a garden rake with the head uppermost and the tines pointing away from you. If it is left lying on the ground it is all too easy to tread on the head and receive a blow to the face or head from the handle.

Shears and secateurs

You may need a pair of garden shears if the site is really overgrown. It may be possible to borrow these at first, but you would do well to invest in some of your own at some point.

Still on the subject of cutting tools, as your first season wears on and lots of growth is produced you are going to need the services of a pair of secateurs, especially if you are going to grow fruit trees or bushes. Always buy the best quality that you can afford – cheaper brands quickly fall apart under heavy use. Secateurs must have a clean cutting action; poorly manufactured sets will tear and bruise the branches, leaving ragged cuts that are wide open to infection. There are two different cutting actions available: one is the anvil type where the cutting blade cuts down on to a flattened edge (the anvil). The problem with these is that after a while the anvil becomes worn and the blade crushes the shoot rather than cutting cleanly through it. By far the best cutting action is provided by by-pass or parrot-bill secateurs, where the blade slices against a flattened edge. As long as the blade is kept sharp and tensioned properly, the pruning cuts are always perfect. A complaint often voiced is that most secateurs are made for right-handed people. Felco (**www.worldoffelco.uk**) produces left-handed secateurs for those who need them.

Clip-on tools

These are becoming more and more popular and the range of attachments available has increased greatly. This system is ideal where storage space is limited, as one handle can become a rake, hoe, cultivator, lawn rake, scarifier, brush, tiller, pruner or pole saw. If a particular attachment becomes worn out or damaged it can quickly and easily be replaced. They are great for sticking in the back of a car if you have to drive to and from the allotment and do not have access to a shed.

Machinery in the garden

Machinery can be a blessing and a curse in the garden. The job to be done has to be big enough to justify the expense of buying or hiring special machinery. Any mechanical equipment used in the garden must be safe and reliable to use. There is nothing more frustrating and time wasting than a machine that will not start or runs erratically.

Strimmers and hedge cutters may take a lot of the backache out of clearing overgrown areas, but they do generate a large amount of rubbish that has to be disposed of. Chippers and shredders will break the debris down into chips that are fine enough to be put on the compost heap or used as a mulch around fruit trees and bushes.

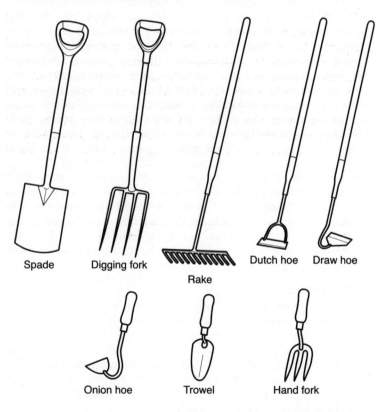

Spade   Digging fork   Dutch hoe   Draw hoe

Rake

Onion hoe   Trowel   Hand fork

figure 1.1 gardening tools

There is no doubting the strength and stamina that is required to hand dig and cultivate a vegetable garden. Rotovating the soil with a machine is much easier than digging it by hand, but in the long term the structure of the soil will be damaged. The regular use of a rotovator will eventually create a hard polished layer, known as a pan, about 30 cm (12 inches) below the surface of the soil. This pan is totally impervious to water, causing any surface irrigation to run off sideways rather than sink into the soil and, equally importantly, preventing water rising upwards through the soil towards the roots of plants. The pan has to be broken up using a subsoiler, which is a kind of plough used to loosen the deeper soil.

Warning!

One machine that must be treated with the utmost respect in the garden is the chainsaw. These machines are perfectly safe in the hands of experts, but in the hands of amateur gardeners they can be lethal. The fact that they can be bought at any garden suppliers creates a false sense of security. Professional gardeners have to undergo long hours of training and examinations to become proficient in their use. If there are any trees in your garden that require the attention of a chainsaw, always send for the experts.

02 soil types

In this chapter you will learn:
- why soil pH is important and how to adjust it
- about the different types of soil and how to recognize them
- how to improve the structure of your soil.

The soil has to provide everything that a plant will need to grow and flourish. A gardener first needs to get the soil into the best possible condition before any seed sowing or planting takes place. Creating a fertile and friable (crumbly) soil is the single most important job in the garden. Do not take it for granted that if you are taking on an existing garden the soil will be fine. You could be inheriting a garden or allotment where the soil is tired out because it has been over-cropped and nothing has been put back into the soil to keep it in good condition. Alternatively, you may be creating a brand new garden around a new home where the soil has been churned up by building machinery and a shallow coating of topsoil has been spread over it for cosmetic purposes.

Soil pH and what it means to the gardener

The term 'soil pH' is used to describe the acidity or alkalinity of the soil. Peaty type soils are acidic, and chalky/lime soils are alkaline. The soil pH is based on a scale of 0 to 14, with pH 7 being neutral. Below pH 7 the soil becomes progressively more acidic and from pH 7 to pH 14 it becomes more alkaline. It is important to know what the pH level of soil is because it will determine the range of plants you will be able to grow in it. For example, fruit trees prefer to be grown on soil which is slightly alkaline, and most garden vegetables grow best in slightly acid soil with a pH of 6.5.

It is easy to discover the pH of the soil using a soil pH testing kit that can be bought from any garden centre. Everything that is needed to carry out the test is included in the kit. A small sample of dry soil is placed in a test tube containing a harmless chemical indicator. The tube is shaken to mix the two together and then the soil and chemical are allowed to settle and separate. A colour-sensitive paper is then dipped into the liquid that forms on top of the soil sample and after a while it will turn either orange/red, indicating acid, or blue/green, indicating alkaline. The degree of acidity or alkalinity of the soil is then indicated by comparing the colour on the paper against the colour chart supplied with the kit. The nearest match will indicate the accurate pH of the soil.

1	2	3	4	5	6	7	8	9	10	11	12	13	14
Acid (*red to orange*)						Neutral	Alkaline (*green to blue*)						
Too acidic to support plants						**Best growing range**	Too alkaline to support plants						

Adjusting the pH of the soil

Generally, most soils are able to grow a wide range of plants and it is only in extreme cases that dramatic corrections have to be made. It is possible to make some small adjustments to the pH levels.

> **Caution**
> When handling lime and sulphur, always wear overalls, gloves and goggles.

Liming the soil

A low pH can be raised by treating the soil with lime. The lime can be applied to the soil in the form of ground limestone, ground chalk, hydrated lime or magnesium limestone. Always use the lime at the recommended rate – do not be tempted to over-apply the lime to the soil. It is best to raise the pH level gradually rather than attempting to do it all at once.

It is only necessary to top-dress the soil with lime until the correct pH has been reached. After this has been achieved, check the pH level occasionally, only correcting it as is required.

Applying powdered sulphur to the soil

It is much more difficult to lower a high soil pH. The regular digging in of organic matter can help to bring it down. However, there will always be the problem of overcoming the alkaline soil water from the surrounding land draining into the plot and constantly raising the pH level. A soil with a high pH can be top-dressed with powdered sulphur to lower the level of alkalinity. Beware, however, as on poorly drained soil sulphur can become toxic to plants. It reacts with the organic material in the soil and produces a gas, which gives off a very unpleasant smell.

Spread the powdered sulphur evenly over the surface of the soil. Work it into the soil using a three- or five-pronged cultivator.

Both the ground limestone and powdered sulphur can be bought from garden centres in carry-home bags.

Top tip

One way to overcome the problems of extremes of pH in a particular area of the garden (very high or very low) is to raise the level of the soil above that of the surrounding area. This will allow better drainage for the more poorly drained acidic soils. The sides of the raised area can be contained using old railway sleepers or second-hand boards. (See Chapter 07 for more information.)

Soil structure

Soil falls into one of five types and each one is quite distinct from the other. These are clay, silty clay, chalky, peat and sandy soils. It is a straightforward enough process to recognize the soil type in your garden. Pick up a handful of the soil and gently rub a small sample of it between your forefinger and thumb. The way it looks and feels will give clues to its structure. The short descriptions listed below should help you to identify your soil.

Clay

This feels sticky to the touch, polishes easily when rubbed between finger and thumb and is easily moulded.

Clay holds more water than other soils, which can lead to waterlogging, making the soil unworkable especially during the winter months. Clay is a cold soil that is slow to warm up in the spring because the water in the soil takes a long time to warm. It is considered to be the heaviest of the soil types. When compared with the lighter sandy soils, it takes four times as much energy to dig a clay soil. All cultivations must be timed carefully to avoid seriously damaging the structure. Autumn digging is always recommended because it exposes the clay soil to the beneficial effects of the winter frosts, but *do not* dig it when it is wet or it will dry into hard unworkable lumps in the spring.

Silt

This is sticky, has a smooth, silky feel when rubbed between forefinger and thumb and is easily moulded.

Silty soils are usually poorly drained because the fine soil particles stick together, retarding the movement of water through the soil. They do not form crumbs easily and this makes them difficult to manage. Silty soil is usually found in land that is near flooding rivers.

Sandy

This feels gritty, does not stain the fingers and is not sticky.

These are the lightest of the soil types and for this reason they can be worked in all weathers. They are free draining, which means that they will warm up very quickly in the spring. The water-holding capacity of sandy soils is very low, so irrigation of the soil is essential to prevent the plants suffering from drought. Sandy soils are considered 'hungry' soils because the nutrients are easily washed out of the soil by water and have to be reapplied for each crop grown. Organic matter is very beneficial as it binds the soil particles together and helps to retain moisture. Pig or cow manure is best, but any form of organic matter is good.

Chalky

When chalky soils are wet they are sticky, and when dry they tend to 'cake', making the soil difficult to manage. Sometimes they will have white flints mixed in with the soil.

Sometimes called calcareous soils, these are formed from chalk or limestone rocks and are therefore alkaline, with a high pH. They can contain up to 40 per cent calcium carbonate. They tend to be very low in organic matter and plant food. They can be improved by incorporating organic matter and fertilizer, especially phosphate. Chalky soils can be very shallow, with only a spit depth of soil over the chalk. To increase the depth of the topsoil, build it up with a 15-cm (6-inch) layer of loam.

Peat

Peat soils are formed from organic matter that has decomposed under waterlogged conditions, so they are acidic, with a low pH. Peat soils have a high water table and have to be drained to become workable. Under extreme conditions the surface of the soil can dry out and become dusty and vulnerable to blowing away in high winds. Although they are formed from organic matter, peat soils have no nutrients in them at all. Their fertility can be improved by using artificial or organic fertilizers.

Top tip

Always keep off the soil when it is waterlogged otherwise it will destroy the soil structure.

03

soil preparation

In this chapter you will learn:
- why digging is important for soil cultivation
- about different methods of cultivation
- why soil preparation is important for growing healthy plants.

A soil has to provide a plant with:

- nutrients
- moisture
- root anchorage.

Soil profile

When you dig a hole or trench in the ground you will notice that the soil changes colour the deeper that you go down. The different coloured bands of soil form what is known as the soil profile. The top layer is the darkest because it is formed from decaying organic matter breaking down in the soil. This layer is the most fertile and is where most of the plants' roots grow. It is called the topsoil. The next layer contains much less organic material and is noticeably less friable. It is usually lighter in colour and is called the subsoil. Beneath the subsoil is the parent soil or bedrock. This layer was laid down millions of years ago and over time has been covered up with the subsoil and topsoil.

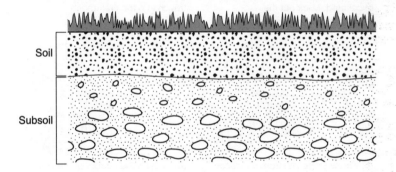

figure 3.1 soil profile

Cultivation

Digging involves the development of the top spit or topsoil into a friable and fertile soil that will produce first-class crops. But it is of no benefit to the gardener to cultivate only the top spit if the subsoil is in poor condition and needs to be improved.

Single digging

This is the practice of cultivating the soil to the depth of a spade (30 cm/12 inches). In single digging the soil is lifted and completely inverted to turn the top layer in and expose the remainder of the soil to the air. Organic matter can also be dug in at this time. The weathering effects of wind, frost and rain will then break the lumps down into a smaller, more crumbly structure.

(a) The first trench has been excavated. Mark out the second trench

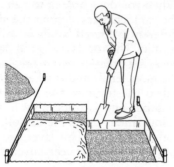

(b) Throw the soil from the second trench into the first trench

(c) Throw loose soil from the second trench to level off the first trench

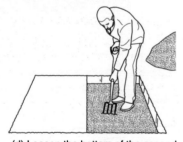

(d) Loosen the bottom of the second trench with a fork. Mark out the next section and repeat the process

figure 3.2 single digging

Double digging

This is a process where the soil is dug out to a depth of two spits. However, this is no longer practised because it is considered too disruptive to the soil and of no real benefit to following crops.

Bastard trenching

This is now the accepted replacement for double digging. It still means opening up a trench 45 cm (18 inches) wide and one spit deep, but instead of digging out the lower layer of the trench, it is simply loosened and not turned over. This is done by driving a digging fork into the full depth of the tines and then levering the fork to and fro. The major benefit of this action is to break up any compaction or pan and allow surface water to penetrate the soil more deeply, while at the same time allowing water from the lower levels of the soil to rise towards the stop spit. It also encourages the roots of plants to develop deeper root systems. Before the trench is backfilled, a 7.5-cm (3-inch) deep layer of organic material can be spread over the bottom of the trench.

Top tip 🍅🍅

It doesn't matter if you don't have enough organic matter to cover the entire vegetable garden. Dig it in the section where it will be of benefit to the crop being grown. Next year move on to another section.

Rough digging/ridging

This is a first-class way of breaking down clay or heavy soils. The soil is left in large lumps or ridges. This allows the water in the soil to drain away from the crest of the ridge, causing it to dry out and to be more easily broken down by winter frosts.

Forking

In this process the soil is not turned over with the fork, but the back of the tines are used to smash the sods into smaller pieces as part of the preparation of a tilth on the soil prior to planting or seed sowing. The garden fork is not used as much as the spade for digging, but it is a useful tool for lightly pricking over the surface of the soil to ease compaction and for improving drainage of sites.

Pronged cultivator

The three- or five-pronged cultivator is a useful tool to knock down the large lumps of soil into smaller crumbs.

Raking

The rake is used to produce the fine tilth that is necessary when preparing seedbeds. As it is drawn across the surface of the soil it knocks the small lumps of soil together, breaking them down into a fine, almost sand-like texture. This fine texture is critical to successful seed sowing because it ensures that the seed and soil are in close contact with each other. If the lumps are too large there are air spaces between the lumps, and if a seed germinates within one of these spaces it could dry out and die. The corner of the rake is also used to produce seed drills; it is drawn slowly along the garden line to create a straight drill.

Hoeing

The single most important use for a garden hoe is to kill and control weeds. There are several types of hoe, the most common being the Dutch hoe. Most of them operate by being pushed forwards and pulled backwards just underneath the surface of the soil. They chop the top of the plant away from the roots; these are both left on the surface of the soil to shrivel and die. The hoe is very good for loosening the compacted surface of the soil.

Draw hoe

The draw hoe is very effective against perennial weeds. It is very sturdy and is used to chop at weeds rather than slide underneath them. It is also a very useful tool to earth up potatoes or draw soil up around the necks of plants.

It cannot be stressed too much just how important thorough soil preparation is to success in the vegetable garden – without it everything will struggle. There will be times when frustration creeps in because of the weather or the lack of time to get jobs done, but never cut corners and take risks with the soil. Most of the digging is carried out during the wintertime when the days are short and the weather is at its meanest, but the golden rule is never, under any circumstances at all, to walk or work on the soil when it is wet or frozen. Even if this means having to hold back until the drying days of the spring, the rewards will be worth the wait.

04

manure, compost and fertilizers

In this chapter you will learn:
- how to make garden compost
- how to construct a wormery
- how to use green manures
- what the major elements in fertilizers are
- the differences between organic and inorganic fertilizers.

Healthy soil will always grow healthy plants. In nature, the fertility and structure of the soil is maintained by the fallen autumn leaves and remains of plant material being broken down and eventually incorporated into the soil via the activity of worms, insects, bacteria and fungi. Even the occasional dead creature will fall to the ground and decompose to make its contribution. It is in this way that the natural balance between a plant's nutritional requirement and the soil's ability to supply it is maintained. Gardening is in some ways an unnatural practice and makes much greater demands on the soil than nature ever will. It is our responsibility to ensure that whatever goodness we take out of the soil by growing crops is put back in. We can do this by feeding the soil with bulky organic matter such as farmyard manure or homemade garden compost – there is no need to use artificial fertilizers to boost the soil's fertility.

Sources of manure

Years ago, the most common source of organic material was well-rotted cow or horse manure. Today these are not so easy to come by as most of us live in towns. There may be a riding school in your local neighbourhood, but even then the quality of the manure is unsatisfactory. The horses of today are fed on 'cake', which does not contain any fibre, and they are also bedded on shredded paper or sawdust. These make a poor substitute for the real thing – strawy manure.

Garden compost

Garden compost should not be confused with the bagged seed and potting composts that are manufactured strictly for plant raising. Garden compost is made from decomposed non-woody plant material. This could be:

- old bedding plants
- prunings
- lawn mowings
- annual weeds
- fruit
- the leaves that have been trimmed from vegetables, either during harvesting or during preparation in the kitchen.

Avoid using:

- the peel from citrus fruits, because these are too acidic
- cooked meats, because these will attract vermin which will be unpleasant for you and your neighbours.

Making a compost heap

To make garden compost, all of the materials have to be stacked in a heap to encourage the breakdown of the vegetation into a dark and crumbly texture. But it is not just a case of throwing everything on top of each other. There are a few simple rules that have to be followed to be a successful composter. The important ingredients in the making of first-class compost are plant waste, air and moisture. It is vitally important to prevent the heap from becoming too wet or too dry because this will stop the rotting-down process. Always make the heap on soil and not on a solid surface such as concrete or tarmac.

The compost heap can either be made as an open pile or, preferably, within a container. Whichever system you choose to use, the heap has to be made in layers. Each layer is 15 cm (6 inches) deep, and each layer has to be 'capped' or covered with a dusting of garden lime (to counter the acidity as the material decomposes) and garden soil (to introduce the bacteria that speed up the breakdown of the heap). There is no need to use proprietary compost accelerators – they are not necessary.

Garden compost is made from annual weeds, grass cuttings and vegetable waste from the garden and kitchen. These are the 'wet' ingredients. They must be mixed with drier material such as shredded paper, cardboard and dried plant remains to create the right balance inside the heap. As each layer is built up, lightly tamp the material down using the back of a garden fork to pack everything together. Take care not to over compact the layer because this will drive out the air trapped in the mixture of vegetative waste.

After a few months, the heap will have shrunk in size as the materials have rotted down. As this happens, all of the vegetation in the heap will begin to pack together, which will in turn stop the decomposition activity because of the lack of air in the compost heap. To revitalize the heap, all of the partially made compost must be dug out of the container onto the ground in front of the heap. It must then be thrown back into the container to begin the final stage of the process. This is where the two-bin method is best because the half-made heap can be thrown into the neighbouring bin and a fresh heap started in the emptied bin.

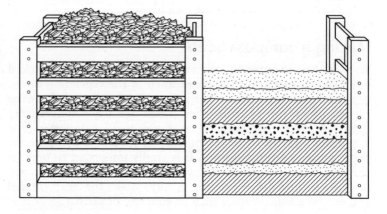

figure 4.1 compost bins

When most of the heap has turned to compost you can remove the top layer to start the next heap. It is always best to have at least two compost heaps, one ready to use and the other in the making.

Leaf mould

Leaf mould should not be confused with garden compost. It is formed by an entirely different process from composting. Compost is the product of *bacteria* breaking down soft vegetative material. Leaf mould is the product of beneficial *fungi* breaking down the leaves to form a dark, peat-like material. Leaf mould is low in nutrients but is a first-class soil conditioner.

The formation of leaf mould is a simple process – in nature, the leaves fall from the trees in autumn, settling on the ground. There, a combination of moisture, fungi and small invertebrates begin to attack the leaf litter, turning it into humus, but you do not need your own personal woods to be able to make leaf mould successfully. All that is required is a cage constructed from galvanized chicken wire or plastic netting. The size of the cage depends on the quantity of leaves that you have at your disposal. However, in practical terms anything larger than 1 metre (10 ft) square can become unmanageable when full. To construct the cage, knock four stout wooden stakes of 150 cm (5 ft) long by 5 cm (0.8 inches) square at least 45 cm (18 inches) into the ground at each corner of the cage. Next, using wire staples or strong nylon string, secure the netting to the stakes to form the enclosure. It makes it easier to empty the stack if one of the sides is hinged and can be used as a door. It is not critical to be able to fill the net at once, but it is best if the task can be completed as soon as possible.

Because moisture plays an important part in the process, it is best if the leaves are collected when they are still wet before putting them into the cage. If this is not possible they will have to be spread out on the ground and well watered using a watering can or hosepipe. If dry leaves are put on the stack they can slow down the process or even bring it to a halt. Create the stack in layers, gently firming each layer. Leave the leaf pile until at least the following season to create beautiful leaf mould that can be spread over the soil as a mulch.

Not all leaves are suitable for making leaf mould – avoid using the tough, leathery types such as plane that will take years to break down, or leaves that are high in toxins such as horse chestnut. Do not use leaves from along side roads that may have been treated with rock salt.

Never, under any circumstances, be tempted to collect leaf mould from the 'wild', such as local woods or forests. When it is in an advanced state of decomposition it will have already entered the ecosystem and be actively involved in supporting wildlife. If you do collect leaves from anywhere except your own garden, always get the permission of the landowner before you start to collect leaves – it may seem petty but a little courtesy goes a long way.

Top tip

If you own a rotary mower with a grass box and have grassed areas covered in leaves, it will make life easier to run the mower over the leaves to collect them. Set the mower to its highest setting and use it just as if cutting the grass. It also helps to speed up the process by chopping the leaves before they are put in the cage.

Worm compost

Another method of producing organic material for the garden is worm composting (vermicomposting). Vermiculture is the rearing of the worms that are used in vermicomposting.

It has long been acknowledged that earthworms are one of the gardener's greatest friends. They are nature's soil builders – they literally eat their way through the soil, digesting nutrients from it and passing the soil out of their bodies, leaving it in an improved state as worm casts. Worms will drag all forms of organic matter, ranging from compost to farmyard manure and leaf mould, down from the surface of the soil to the lower levels where it becomes converted into humus. They are natural composters, working all the time at breaking down organic matter and converting it into a nutrient-rich material.

The hundreds of tunnels that the earthworms create as they burrow through the soil also help to let in rain and air, and the worms' bodies exude a lubricating fluid that helps to bind soil particles together, forming them into crumbs. Once you have a healthy worm population it is a sure indication that you have created a healthy, living soil. Worm casts are far more fertile than the surrounding soil – they have higher levels of nitrogen, phosphates and potassium, and it is this ability to turn organic waste into a high-grade compost and fertilizer that makes worm composting such an attractive proposition for the gardener.

A wormery allows you to use worms to convert household kitchen waste, paper and cardboard into a useful compost and plant fertilizer that can be used in the kitchen garden.

Constructing a wormery

It is important that the wormery is sited where it is sheltered from direct sunlight and rain; worms prefer a warm but not too hot environment and any rain getting inside would cool the compost, which will make the worms sluggish.

The wormery can be any suitable container that can house the worms and hold the plant waste as they break it down to form compost. The container can be a factory-made article or something as basic as a bucket that has been modified for the job; dustbins are too deep to be used, as will be explained later in the text.

Wormeries can be made of wood or plastic, but wood is a better insulator and is a more suitable material when building your own DIY bin. The wormery itself has to be constructed in layers: each layer consists of a shallow tray to hold the household waste and the worms. Each tray must have a perforated base to allow the casts to fall through; the wooden trays can be fitted with a wire mesh. Each tray or chamber only needs to be 40 cm (16 inches) deep and about 60 cm (9 inches) square.

The trays are made shallow because the worms used in vermicomposting (see below) are surface feeders and are only able to work in the upper layers of the soil. As each tray begins to fill up with composted material another tray is placed on top of it to create the next batch of compost. The worms will work their own way from the lower tray and into the upper tray – as each tray is completed so another is added. It is important to ensure that the bottom of the uppermost tray is always in close contact with the top of the compost in the lower tray, as any gap between them will prevent the upward movement of the worms. Remember that worms do not have legs – they cannot jump! Usually there is no need to go any higher than three or four trays. Just try to ensure that there is a movement of the solids and liquids through the wormery.

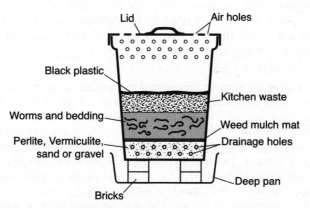

figure 4.2 a wormery made from a bucket

As well as converting the waste into solid matter, the worms create a liquid which has to be held in a reservoir of some description. The factory-produced wormeries have a tank built into the base tray that is fitted with a drainage tap to draw off the liquid. With a DIY wormery you could use a deep pan that is removable to collect the liquids.

The worms

The most commonly used worms in wormeries are *Eisenia fetida*, better known as brandlings or tiger worms. These are the worms used by anglers. They are also the ones that are always found in heaps of old stable manure. Tiger worms are very distinctive in appearance; they have pinky-red and yellow bands along their body that give them their name. They also reproduce and grow quite rapidly and this is what makes them so attractive to use in wormeries. Other types of worms that are used in vermiculture are *Eisenia andrei* and *Dendrobaena*.

Getting the wormery started

The first stage in setting up the wormery is to place a layer of bedding material for the newly introduced worms over the bottom of the first tray. This can be made from black and white newspapers torn into 25-mm (1-inch) wide strips and thoroughly soaked, then allowed to drain until they feel as damp as a wrung-out flannel or sponge.

• Fill the first chamber with the moistened newspaper.
• Add a few handfuls of garden soil and the waste material (worm food).
• Next, introduce the worms to the mixture.
• Finally, cover the tray with a piece of old carpet or a few sheets of newspaper to keep the chamber warm, and wait for the worms to set to work.

The worms are hungry eaters and can consume more than their own weight each day. It will take about 0.5 kg (1 lb) of worm food to get started. Do not be tempted to add too much kitchen waste to the bin at first. Let the worms acclimatize to their new surroundings and gradually increase the amounts as they become more active. As a rough guide 0.5 kg (1 lb) of worms will consume 250 gm (0.5 lb) of waste material each day; the amount of waste will have to be increased as the size of the worm population increases. The worms need time to adjust to any new food and it does help them if the food is shredded into small pieces. Controlling the temperature inside the wormery is a critical factor for maximizing the worm activity – a temperature of around 20°C (68°F) is the ideal. Just like us, the worms' health will benefit from a little fibre, so include torn-up egg boxes or the cardboard centres from toilet and kitchen paper rolls. After a while the conditions inside the wormery can become acidic: to counterbalance this use a fortnightly dressing of lime mix, which also introduces a little grit to the soft fibre diet. Worms, just like chickens, need the grit to clean their gizzards out and keep them clear for grinding food.

Worms are able to digest all of the following:

- vegetable peelings
- apple and pear remains
- tea leaves/bags
- coffee grounds
- bread
- flower heads
- soft leaves (not stems or stalks)
- shredded paper
- black and white newspaper torn into 25-mm (1-inch) strips.

Crushed eggshells are excellent to use to counter any acidity in the wormery.

Food *not* to feed to worms:

- meat, bones and greasy foods
- fats and dairy products
- twigs, branches and hard leaves (e.g. holly)
- dog and cat faeces
- citrus fruits and peels as they are too acidic
- rubber and plastics.

A well-managed wormery should not pose any problems at all. There should not be any unpleasant smells or swarms of flies to put up with. If there are, it is a sign that something is going wrong inside the bin. If the bin smells it could be for several reasons:

- Poor air circulation – put fresh *dry* bedding material under and over the worms. Do not feed the worms for two weeks.
- Exposed waste scraps in the bin – cover the waste and the worms with fresh bedding material.
- Uncompostable materials in the bin – these must be removed.

Dead and dying worms in the wormery will cause the greatest alarm. This could be happening for several reasons:

- They are not getting enough food – bury the food more deeply in the bedding.
- Conditions inside the bin may be too dry – add water to the box until it feels damp.

- The compost could be too wet – add fresh bedding.
- Too many fluctuating temperature levels will kill the worms, so always avoid rapid changes of temperatures in and around the wormery bin.

It is important to the health of the worm colony that the finished compost is not allowed to build up inside the wormery and that fresh bedding material is introduced at least twice each year.

Harvesting the compost

After six months or so the bedding should have been eaten and the first harvest of crumbly, brown worm compost should be ready for harvesting. Stop any feeding in the two weeks leading up to the chosen harvesting time. The compost can be collected in two ways.

1 Push all of the compost across to one side of the tray, at the same time removing any large pieces of undigested waste matter. Put fresh bedding and food on the empty side of the tray. After this time, only add waste to the fresh side of the tray – this is to encourage the worms to leave the fully composted half and to move over and populate the freshly replenished side of the tray. When this has happened the compost can be harvested and the emptied half of the tray replenished with new bedding and food. Cover the earlier half to dry it out so as to encourage some of the worms to repopulate the fresh half and gradually return the tray to normal management. This method is suitable where there is only one chamber.

2 If you have a stack of multiple chambers this second method may be simpler. Empty the entire contents of the tray on to a ground sheet. Make several cone-shaped piles out of the compost. The worms will move away from the light to the bottom of each pile. Remove the compost from the top of the piles, separating the decomposed material from the partly broken down material. The worms will continue to work their way to the bottom of each pile. Repeat and continue with this method until all of the compost has been harvested and the worms are safely left at the bottom of each pile. Gather up the worms to restock the wormery. It is inevitable that there will be worms in the compost, but do not worry about this.

How to use the worm compost and liquid

The worm compost can be used straight away or stored for future use. It is more concentrated than other types of compost, therefore it should be used sparingly to obtain the best results and avoid any possible damage to plants. It can be used as a 5-cm (2-inch) deep mulch around plants or incorporated into the soil before sowing or planting takes place. Another application is as a base dressing for pot plants: spread it over the surface of the compost and each time the pot is watered the plant gets a liquid feed. It can be used as part of a potting compost in the recipe as follows:

- one part worm compost
- three parts potting compost or three parts soil and sand mixed in equal measure

OR

- drain or pour the liquid out and store it in a clearly marked container and dilute it at a rate of 10:1 and use it as a liquid fertilizer.

Green manure

Using a 'green manure' is an alternative method of improving the structure and fertility of the soil. No animal manures of any description are involved in the process and it is a first-class substitute where circumstances make it difficult to obtain the real thing or you prefer not to use farmyard manure on your garden. Green manuring is the practice of sowing a fast-growing and beneficial crop in the soil that has to be cut down and dug into the soil at a later date. Green manuring can be carried out either during your initial soil preparations, or following the clearing of a piece of ground of a crop after harvesting. It is a system that has been used by farmers for centuries and gardeners have adapted it to meet their own particular needs.

Types of green manure

There are two groups of green manure that you can use on your vegetable plot, they are the 'fixers' and 'lifters'. The fixers are members of the legume family that have the ability to absorb free nitrogen found in the atmosphere and store it in nodules/growths on their roots. The entire crop is then dug back into the ground and releases the nitrogen into the soil to the later benefit of any crop that is grown on that particular piece of land. This is why brassicas, which are leafy vegetables that have a high demand for nitrogen, always follow on from peas and beans in any crop rotation plan.

Lifters are crops such as rye grass or mustard, which can absorb or 'lift' any excess nitrogen from the soil and store it within their leaves. When they are eventually dug into the soil, the nitrogen they contain will then help to balance the loss of nitrogen to the soil when breaking down the green leaves. They also produce extensive fibrous root systems that will improve the structure of the soil when they are dug back in. As well as maintaining the soil in first-class condition green manures can be used to smother and control weeds.

This is a crude description of a very sophisticated operation, but it is hoped that you can now understand how to boost nitrogen levels to the benefit of the following crop, or how to reduce nitrogen levels if they are too high and likely to produce soft, large, leafy growth on a root crop such as carrots. Where the soil fertility is acceptable but it still lacks organic matter, bulky green manures such as rye grass are excellent for improving the humus levels in the soil.

Benefits of using green manure

If the soil is left bare for any length of time, rain will wash out (leach) precious plant nutrients from the soil. One consequence of the leaching process is the pollution of streams, rivers and other watercourses with a range of dilute fertilizers that encourage rank, lush growth in water plants. It also poses serious health problems for a variety of water creatures. Through the use of green manures the gardener can store these free nutrients within the body of the plant and help to prevent an environmental headache. A covering of green manure will protect the soil against damage from the elements.

The major benefits of using green manures are:

1 Soil fertility is improved by preventing the leaching of valuable nutrients from the soil.
2 They store and return nutrients and organic material to the soil.

3 The incorporation of the bulky green manures improves the 'crumb structure' of the soil, allowing air spaces to be created in between the individual lumps of soil.

4 Water retention and penetration are improved because of the more open soil structure. Also, the decomposed plant material increases the humus content of the soil, which acts as a sponge, absorbing and storing the water.

5 Any uncovered areas of soil are protected, especially over the winter. The covering of a green manure prevents the bare earth from being compacted by heavy rains and also from the eroding effects of strong winds and rain.

There is not one green manure to suit all occasions. You will have to choose one that best meets your particular requirements. Any green manuring programme must fit into the crop rotation plan of the garden. There two main seasons of use, summer and winter.

Summer green manures

These are fast-growing and fleshy annuals. They are the types of crops that will absorb free nitrogen in the soil. They can also act as a neutral crop on ground that is being rested in between crops and, importantly, they will also suppress weed growth.

Summer is the best time of the year to use green manures to increase the organic content of the soil. The constant cropping of the soil depletes it of humus and nutrients, and it is vital that these are replaced. The best time to sow a summer green manure is in the spring. It is able to establish quickly and in a good summer the green manure crop will be ready to dig into the soil within three months of sowing.

Winter green manures

Any part of the vegetable garden that is not required to grow a winter crop can be over sown with a winter green manure. As well as preventing the loss of valuable nutrients from the soil, a winter green manure also affords the soil's surface much-needed protection against the eroding effects of winter winds and rain. Winter green manures have to be sown by the early autumn and most of them are nitrogen lifters. If you intend to use a nitrogen fixer such as clover this will need to be sown by September at the latest because they need warmer conditions in which to grow. The winter green manures are dug in during the spring.

Suitable green manures

Summer

Phacelia – nitrogen lifter. Quick to establish and is mature in three months. It grows vigorously, which makes it a good weed suppressor, and it develops an extensive root system that improves the soil structure. It must be dug into the soil before it sets seed otherwise it could become a weed problem in itself. Its blue flowers also attract beneficial insects such as bees, hoverflies and wasps.

Buckwheat – nitrogen lifter. Vigorous and quick to establish, it is ready in about three months. It is also a good weed suppressor but because it produces a shallow root system it does not appreciate dry or waterlogged conditions. If it is cut down again it will re-grow, making a living mulch, but it will not survive frosty weather. It breaks down quite soon after digging in. One other benefit of using buckwheat is its ability to search for, lift and store any free phosphates in the soil. Sow April onwards, 1 cm (0.5 inches) deep.

Clover – nitrogen fixer. The true aristocrat of the green manure kingdom, famous for its legendary nitrogen-fixing properties. Although clover is slow to establish it will grow quite rapidly and is ready to dig in around three months after sowing. It produces masses of foliage and deep penetrating roots that can reach right down to the subsoil. It must be well dug in to prevent it re-growing among the following crop. Sow April–September, 1 cm (0.5 inches) deep on a well-prepared seedbed as soon as the soil has warmed up.

Mustard – nitrogen lifter. Another famous green manure that can be used to smother weeds. It also reduces wireworm infestations on freshly broken grassland. It is best used between the harvesting of the summer crops and the sowing of a winter green manure. It grows quickly, producing a mass of foliage in around ten weeks, but it must be dug in before it produces flowers and becomes too woody. Remember that mustard is a member of the brassica family so its use must fit in with the rotation programme.

Winter

Rye – nitrogen lifter. Excellent at storing any free nitrogen in the soil in readiness for the following crop. It is hardy enough to grow under cold conditions and will establish quickly, smothering weeds and covering the soil's surface. Growth speeds up in the spring, producing more bulk to dig back into the soil. Sow from mid-September onwards, lightly raking into the surface of the soil.

Vetch – nitrogen fixer. To gain the most benefit from this hardy winter legume it has to be sown by mid-September. It has to be dug back into the soil during the late spring to be followed by a summer crop.

Phacelia – nitrogen lifter. Hardy enough to withstand most winters if it is sown by the end of September. Phacelia will provide good ground cover. It will respond to the warmer weather of spring, producing more bulky growth. It is treated in the same way as summer-sown phacelia.

The management of green manures

Soil preparation – Rake and firm the soil to produce a fine tilth.

Seed sowing – The seed can either be sown in drills/rows or broadcast (thrown loosely by hand) over the surface of the soil. In both cases the seed must just be raked into the surface of the soil.

Aftercare – Water as required until the plants are established, and the seeds must be protected against birds. Little else is required.

Cutting down –There are a few tasks that have to be completed before the green manure can be dug into the soil. First, all of the top growth has to be cut down. This can be done using garden shears, a sickle or simply chopping it down with the blade of a spade. Next, as the foliage lies on the surface of the soil it has to be chopped into smaller pieces to make it easier for the soil to break it down. A sharp garden spade is the ideal tool for this job. Allowing the chopped foliage to wilt for a day or two will make it easier to dig in the manure.

Digging in – The green manure is dug in using a garden spade. It may be easier to dig a trench first and then turn the soil into it, taking great care to completely invert the soil so that the roots are facing upwards. Chop at the root ball with the spade to speed up the breaking-down process. Carry on across the plot until all of the green manure is well incorporated into the soil.

Remember that the green manure must be cut down and dug into the soil at least two to three weeks before you want to sow or plant on the site. This is to allow the soil to stabilize itself after the process of breaking down the fresh foliage has been carried out.

Fertilizers

Most plants obtain their nutrients from the soil. They are absorbed through the roots and are then used by the plants to build up the cells that grow into the stems, leaves, shoots, flowers and fruits that we will eventually eat. Technically the nutrients that are important to promote healthy growth in plants fall into two categories, the 'major' elements that are the chief nutrients required by plants, and the 'minor' or 'trace' elements that are found in smaller quantities in the soil. Most soils have adequate levels of trace elements within them, but the major elements are used up quite rapidly when soils have crops grown on them on a regular basis. Farmyard manure and other sources of organic material cannot be relied upon entirely to replace the major elements that are lost. To do this the gardener has to use additional fertilizers to top up the soil.

The major elements in fertilizers

These are more commonly known by their initials: N for nitrogen, P for phosphate and K for potassium.

Nitrogen (N)

Nitrogen is found in the organic matter in the soil and air. It is required in large amounts for all of the main growth processes in plants. It promotes growth and gives stems and leaves their dark green colour.

A lack of nitrogen causes stunted growth and plants appear pale green and look unhealthy. Too much nitrogen will result in soft, sappy growth that is vulnerable to attack from pests and diseases. An excess of nitrogen can also delay flowering and the ripening of fruit. A deficiency of nitrogen is more of a problem on wet, poorly drained, cold soils and those that are lacking in organic matter.

Nitrogen is required by all leafy crops.

Phosphorus (P)

Phosphorus is found in the organic and mineral matter in the soil. It is vital for rapid formation of a plant's root system. It combines with nitrogen in the development of sturdy, healthy plants. Phosphorus also promotes the early ripening of crops.

A lack of phosphorus results in poor root systems and dull green leaves. A deficiency of phosphorus is more likely to occur in soil that is low in organic matter and on clay-type soils.

Phosphorus is beneficial to leguminous crops.

Potassium (K)

Potassium is found in the organic and mineral matter in the soil. It controls the quality of a crop. It is essential to the development of strong healthy plants, because it promotes disease resistance.

Potassium deficiency results in stunted plants and blue-green leaves. Potassium deficiency is more of a problem on sandy or chalk soils.

It is of great benefit to root crops such as beetroot and carrots.

There are two types of fertilizer available to the gardener: organic or inorganic. Both will succeed in replacing any nutrients lost from the soil.

Inorganic/artificial fertilizers

These, by definition, are not of an organic origin; they do not contain any animal or plant waste products. Inorganic fertilizers are more familiarly known as straight, bagged, chemical or artificial fertilizers. They are produced chemically in factories or are the by-products of an industrial process. Others are manufactured from crude deposits that are found all over the world.

How artificial fertilizers work

Artificial fertilizers are specifically designed to boost the fertility levels of the soil, so creating greater growth and an increase in crop yields. They are manufactured to replace the three major elements N-P-K that are lost to the soil in sustaining the regular and heavy cropping of land. Each individual element will only provide one particular plant food. Therefore, to provide a more balanced fertilizer product, the three elements of N-P-K are mixed to supply the correct levels of nutrients for a variety of crops. These are known as compound fertilizers, and probably the most famous of these is National Growmore, now known as Growmore, which was developed during the Second World War to provide a balanced artificial fertilizer that suited most crops. It has more than proved its worth and is still in use today.

Because artificial fertilizers are much more concentrated than animal manure or compost they must be applied at a lower rate than organic manures. It is important to follow rigorously the manufacturer's instructions regarding application rates to prevent any serious damage to the soil and crop being grown. The application of a fertilizer to the soil before any sowing or planting takes place is called a 'base dressing', and the application of fertilizer to a growing crop is called a 'top dressing'.

Because artificial fertilizers are concentrated salts, great care must be taken not to allow any of the fertilizer to fall on the foliage of the crop because it will damage (scorch) the leaves.

Disadvantages of artificial fertilizers

Artificial fertilizers are a great aid to encouraging plant growth, but their prolonged use will eventually destroy the soil structure, leading to a loss of crops. Artificial fertilizers on their own should not be regarded as a substitute for animal manures and compost. They do not provide or return any kind of organic matter to the soil. To avoid any serious deterioration to the soil, careful monitoring of the growth of crops must be carried out to determine when to use organic matter.

Fertilizers that have been stored under poor conditions for a long time become lumpy and it is important that they are crushed into a fine powder before using. These lumps will weigh more than the recommended rate per square metre or yard.

Organic fertilizers/manures

Farmyard manures (FYM) consist of a mixture of the urine and dung of farm animals with the litter used for their bedding, which can be straw, wood shavings or sawdust, and because of this is a very variable product. It is, however, well balanced in nitrogen and potassium but low in phosphates. FYM will supply humus to the soil and supply a few trace elements. It is a first-class soil conditioner.

Storing and stacking FYM

Farmyard manure should never be used new or fresh. It must be stacked and allowed to break down into a crumbly texture, similar to coarse compost or well-rotted wood chips. During this storage period there is a great danger of valuable nutrients being washed out (leaching away) by exposure to rain. To prevent this from happening the manure must be covered with a waterproof sheet or stacked under cover. The heap or stack undergoes a similar breaking-down process to the compost heap and should be managed in much the same way.

Poultry manure

Many gardeners keep chickens or know somebody who does, especially on allotment sites. Poultry manure is about 2.5 times the strength of FYM and must be used with care. If used on land that is intended for young seedlings it should be applied at least two weeks before any sowing or transplanting takes place. Always take care to store the manure in bags somewhere dry – it must never be allowed to get wet. Poultry manure is probably best used as an activator for the compost heap.

Substitutes for manure

These days it is almost impossible to buy farmyard manure, so gardeners have to consider suitable alternatives. These could be woodchips/shreddings, spent mushroom compost, seaweed or, a product that is now becoming more available, municipal green waste. All of the above are clean and easy to use; there may be a cost involved, but some local authorities give their green waste away for free if you are prepared to collect and bag it yourself. They will all help to build up the humus levels in the soil.

Concentrated organic fertilizers

These are the organic alternatives to artificial fertilizers, and they are used in just the same way to maintain the fertility levels of the soil. They do not supply the plant food directly in themselves but give up their nutrients as they decompose in the soil. For this reason they can be slower acting than their chemical cousins. The nutrients in organic fertilizers are fairly concentrated, so they must be used at a much lower rate that bulky organic manure or compost. The usual dosage rate is 60 gm (2 oz) to 150 gm (5 oz) per square metre or yard, depending on the crop being grown. Organic fertilizers are clean and safe to use in the garden, and an accidental over application will not result in any long-lasting damage to the soil or plants. Because they have to break down in the soil they act as a slow-release fertilizer and one application can sustain a crop throughout the growing season. This makes them very economical to use in the garden.

Even though organic fertilizers are made from animal and plant residues they are not able to form humus in the soil. They must not be used mistakenly as a substitute for bulky organic matter.

A selection of organic fertilizers

Blood, fish and bone supplies nitrogen.

Bone meal supplies phosphates and a little nitrogen to the soil.

Dried blood supplies nitrogen and some phosphates.

Hoof and horn supplies nitrogen and smaller amounts of phosphates.

Pelleted poultry manure is strong and best used as an activator for the compost heap.

Seaweed is worth considering in coastal areas, but great care must be taken not to over-farm it. It decomposes very quickly in the soil so it must be used almost immediately.

Bonfire ash is high in potassium, is soluble and quick acting. It must always be stored under cover to keep it dry until required for use. Burnt ivy ash is a good source of phosphates.

05

seed sowing and plant raising

In this chapter you will learn:
- how to sow seed under glass inside
- how to prepare a seedbed outdoors
- how and when to transplant young plants.

Seed sowing is the first step towards raising vegetable plants, so it is important to make every effort to ensure that only the best-quality materials are used throughout the process.

The seed companies only offer healthy, viable seed that has to be produced to the highest standards possible. They have to demonstrate to the appropriate authorities that the germination rate complies with the legal standards required. It is usually the fault of the gardener if the seeds fail to germinate.

The two main methods of raising vegetable plants are:

1 **Under glass** from seeds that are sown in small trays or pots very early in the year. This usually means having to use a greenhouse or windowsill.
2 **Outdoors** from seed that is sown later on in the open ground on a prepared seedbed.

Each method has its own merits and it is up to the gardener to choose the most suitable for the crop being grown. Not everyone will have access to a greenhouse and while windowsills are a useful place to raise plants, the space available and the poor quality of light they offer is a factor that must be taken into consideration.

If the guidelines below are followed then there should be no disappointments when sowing seeds.

• Always use fresh new seed-sowing compost that has been produced especially for the new season. If the bag containing the compost looks old and faded do not even consider buying it. It is obviously a left-over from the previous season and will be useless.

• Only use new or washed seed trays or pots to prevent any possible attack from pests or diseases. Biodegradable plastic trays and pots are so cheap it is well worth considering buying brand new for each new season.

• The most common cause of seeds failing to germinate is their being covered too deeply. To help to overcome this problem it is best to use fine grade vermiculite, which is heat-expanded clay, to cover the seed when using pots or trays. Seed needs to be covered to a depth that is twice its diameter. This rule applies under glass or outdoors in the open ground.

Provided that warmth and moisture can be made available there should be no problems in raising a bountiful harvest.

Sowing in pots and trays indoors

There are several advantages to starting plants from seed early in the year.

- Varieties of vegetables that require a long growing season, such as onions, can be sown as early as December to grow on and then be transplanted to the open ground the following April.
- It allows you to get the season off to an early start by producing young plants that are grown on under glass to be planted out in the open ground when the weather warms up or under the protection of cloches or frames.
- Tender varieties of vegetables that are vulnerable to late frosts, such as marrows, courgettes, French and runner beans are better sown under protection and transplanted after the last frost in your region.

Equipment needed:

- fresh new seed
- seed trays (boxes) or small flower pots
- fresh seed-sowing compost/vermiculite or pearlite
- plant labels and pencil
- watering can with a fine brass rose.

The timing of the sowing of vegetable seeds early in the season is critical to their success. They will require a temperature of 18°C to 21°C (64°F to 70°F) to germinate, and the most economical way of providing this is with a small electric propagator fitted with a thermostatic control. If funds do not allow this then the airing cupboard can be used, but remember to check the seeds each day, because they must be brought into the light as soon as they begin to germinate. It is only necessary to use a propagator in the early part of the year (January until March). By then the greenhouse, warmed by the sun, will be comfortable enough to accommodate the sowing of most seeds without having to use artificial heat.

The size of pot or tray used to sow the seed in will depend on the size of the seed and the number of plants required. As a rule a 9-cm (3.5-inch) pot will provide around 30 seedlings, which is more than enough for early season plant raising. For seed sowing it is not necessary to use containers that are more than 5 cm (2 inches) deep; for pricking out the trays should be 7.5 cm (3 inches) deep.

Overfill the container with seed compost that has been fluffed up to get air into it. (Never use compost taken directly from the bag. It will be a compacted and airless lump.) Remove the excess compost by drawing a length of wood (a 30-cm/12-inch ruler is perfect for the job) across the top of the container to create a level surface. Gently press the compost using a presser especially made for the job or the bottom of a flowerpot, to leave a 6-mm (¼-inch) rim below the top of the pot/tray. Always water the container at this stage using a watering can that is fitted with a fine brass rose. Leave the container to drain for at least half an hour before sowing the seed. If seed is sown directly on to the soaking wet surface it may rot. Large seed such as broad beans and peas can be individually sown in pots or modules.

Different types of compost:

- soil/loam based – John Innes
- peat based – Levington
- coir composts
- wood waste products/straw.

There are three grades of John Innes (J.I.P.) composts available:

1 J.I.P. No 1 has a low level of nutrients and is suitable for the pricking out and short-term growing on of young seedlings in trays or pots.
2 J.I.P. No 2 has nutrients that are twice as strong as J.I.P. No 1 and is suitable for the medium-term growing of pot plants or using in hanging baskets and tubs.
3 J.I.P. No 3 is three times as strong as J.I.P. No 1. It is really only suitable for the long-term growing of trees and shrubs in containers.

Top tip

Open new bags of seed and potting composts a day or so before they are required to be used. This will allow the compost to 'breathe' and release the build-up of any gases formed from the fertilizers contained in the compost.

Sow the seeds evenly and thinly over the surface of the compost and lightly cover them with sieved compost, pearlite or vermiculite. Cover the container with black plastic or a sheet of glass and place in a heated propagator. When the seedlings emerge, move them immediately into a well-lit position at a temperature of 15°C to 18°C (59°F to 64°F).

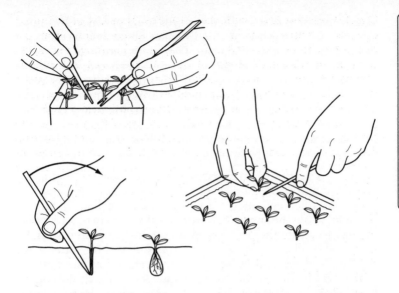

figure 5.1 pricking out seedlings

Prick out the seedlings as soon as they are large enough to hold. Handle them by their seed leaves and place them into trays or pots filled with potting compost containing more and stronger nutrients. Sufficient space has to be found to grow the plants on until planting out time. They are then left to grow at a cool temperature, as close as possible to 10°C (50°F).

Before the plants can be safely planted out in the garden they need to be hardened off. This procedure begins two weeks before the anticipated planting-out date. You can use an unheated greenhouse or frames for this purpose.

At all stages of the process, keep the plants growing – do not allow them to suffer a check by delaying pricking out, potting on or transplanting.

Sowing seed outdoors

From March onwards the soil has usually warmed up enough to be able to sow and plant directly into the soil. Check the temperature of the soil using a soil thermometer – it needs to be at least 7°C (45°F) before seed sowing or transplanting can go ahead. If temperatures are a little on the cool side then cloches or frames can be called into action to warm the soil, but they must be set up at least ten days before the ground is required.

The preparation of a seedbed requires some patience. It is not a job that can be rushed. It usually takes about one week to get the soil in the right condition. The combination of the extra warmth of the sun and the winds of March quickly dry the surface of the soil, telling you that it is safe to walk on. Start by breaking up the lumps of soil created through winter digging by using a three-pronged cultivator. Repeat the job over a couple of days, finally using a garden rake to create a fine tilth on the surface of the soil. At the same time, a base dressing of pelleted poultry manure can be applied all over the area of the seedbed.

To create a neat finish to everything a garden line and measuring board should be used to set out the sowing drills. Set out two sticks at either end of the row and pull the line as taut as possible. Draw the corner of a garden rake or a small stick along the line to create the drill. Stand on the line to keep it straight. If the soil conditions are very dry it is best to dribble water along the length of the drill using a watering can. Allow the water to drain away before sowing the seed and closing the drill using the back of the head of the rake. After the drill is closed, use the head of the rake to tamp the loose earth flat and then lightly drag the rake along the line of the drill to finish the job off.

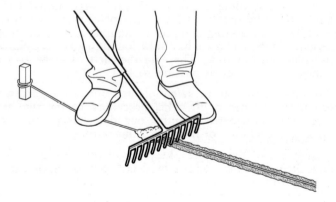

figure 5.2 making a seed drill in open ground

Small seed such as lettuce and carrot can be sown thinly along the entire length of the drill and thinned later. Larger seed, such as beetroot and parsnip, can be spaced evenly along the drill and thinned to one as soon as they are ready to be grown on and planted out after the threat of frost has gone.

Transplanting in the open ground

Always avoid transplanting on hot, sunny days: the transplants will only suffer in the heat and inevitably run to seed later on. Always choose a cool, dull, overcast day to carry out the job.

Before lifting any plants, water along the rows an hour or two earlier. This will ensure that the intended transplants are well charged with water, which will help them survive the trauma of the move.

Carefully dig the plants out of the soil using a hand trowel; try to retain a soil ball around each plant to minimize any damage to the delicate roots. Always place the plants in a tray or box and cover them with a damp cloth to prevent them from drying out.

Take out a hole large enough to accommodate the root system without cramping it. Fill the hole with water, allowing it to soak away before replanting the young plants. Refill around the roots, gently firming the soil, and water once more overhead to settle the soil, using a can with a fine brass rose. There should be no need to water the plant again until it has re-rooted and begun to grow once more.

Soil germination temperatures

Variety	Soil temperature	Days to germination
Beans	22–25°C (75–80°F)	7
Beetroot	23°C (75°F)	7–14
Broccoli	17–23°C (65–75°F)	5–10
Brussels sprouts	20–23°C (68–75°F)	5–10
Cabbage	20–23°C (68–75°F)	5–10
Carrot	23°C (75°F)	12–15
Cauliflower	17–23°C (65–75°F)	5–10
Endive	21–23°C (70–75°F)	10–14
Kale	21–23°C (70–75°F)	5–10
Kohlrabi	21–22°C (70–75°F)	5–10
Lettuce	17–23°C (65–70°F)	7–10
Onions	21–23°C (70–75°F)	10–14

Variety	Soil temperature	Days to germination
Parsnip	21°C (70°F)	14–21
Peas	17–23°C (65–75°F)	7–14
Radish	17–23°C (65–75°F)	5–7
Spinach	21°C (70°F)	7–14
Swiss chard	21–23°C (70–75°F)	7–14
Turnip	17–23°C (65–75°F)	7–14

06

watering

In this chapter you will learn:
- how soil structure affects the water supply to plants
- why artificial irrigation can be ineffective
- how to conserve the moisture content of the soil.

More plants are killed because they are over-watered than because they are under-watered. The watering of plants is a skill that has to be mastered as quickly as possible in order to grow plants successfully.

Under glass

The amount of water that a plant receives depends entirely upon its size and rate of growth. It is all too common a fault among gardeners to water pots and trays every day without checking on the condition of the compost first. Plants do not like having their roots sitting in cold and over-wet compost even for a short period of time. If the surface of the compost is dry but just underneath it feels damp there is no need to water. The appearance of the plants is a good a guide as anything: if the plants look a little limp they need watering. Choose a warm, sunny day to do this if possible, and try to water the plants early in the morning. This will allow any excess water to evaporate in the warmth of the sun.

Try to create a fresh atmosphere in the greenhouse by linking the watering regime to the careful management of the ventilation. On sunny days during the early months of the year the temperatures under glass can soar to a high of 27°C (80°F) even if there is a frost outside. This can often result in the soft young plants suddenly having to cope with desert-like conditions. Open the top and side ventilators just enough to allow the hot, dry air to escape. This will help to lower the temperatures, but the air will still be dangerously dry and pose a real threat to the wellbeing of the plants. To help revive the atmosphere inside the greenhouse, water along the paths, really giving them a good soaking, and as the water evaporates it will put moisture back into the air, making conditions much more comfortable for the inhabitants. Watering the pathways will also help to cool down the greenhouse – it should smell and feel just as it does after a rain shower on a summer's day. Always be sure to close all ventilators and doors by the middle of the afternoon to trap the heat and keep the greenhouse warm overnight.

There will be times when the greenhouse has to be left unattended for most of the working day. To help get around this problem there are one or two greenhouse accessories that can be brought into action. Automatic openers can be fitted to the ventilators; these can be set to open and close at any desired temperature. A capillary mat can be laid over the staging to keep all of the pots and trays supplied with water. The capillary matting is made from a water retentive material and when the pots and trays are placed on it they are able to take up water through the drainage holes in the bottom of the pots. The one disadvantage of capillary matting is that it can encourage the growth of green algae on its surface.

Cloches

The same rules apply to the watering of plants being grown under cloches. Most cloches are designed so that any rainwater will run down the sides and keep the soil moist through capillary action.

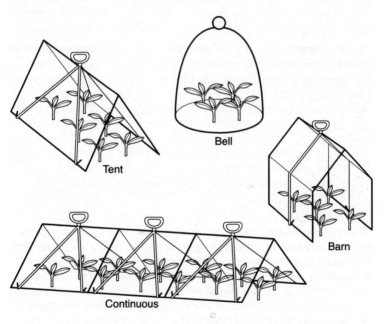

Tent

Bell

Barn

Continuous

figure 6.1 types of cloches

Outside

Water is lost from soil through the leaves of plants, and the rate at which it evaporates from them will depend upon the weather. On hot sunny days or under strong windy conditions the water is sucked out of the leaves and is lost into the atmosphere at a greater rate than it can be replaced via the roots. This causes the plants to display shrivelled or wilting foliage and any attempt to overcome this by simply pouring endless amounts of water over the plant is doomed to failure. It will only damage the soil structure, create airless, waterlogged conditions around the root system and result in the plants being lost to root-rot diseases.

All plants depend upon a reliable source of water being available to them throughout their growing lives. This fact is crucial to the production of crisp, succulent and flavoursome crops. Do not over-water or allow the plants to dry out as this will result in stunted plants with tough leaves and a fibrous texture.

The first step towards providing an adequate water supply is to create a soil reservoir, which will store and release the water as the growing plants demand it. Heavy soils can hold more water than the lighter sandy soils, but heavier soil has to have sufficient drainage to remove excess water and the lighter soils will have to have organic matter dug into them regularly to increase their water-holding capacity. Sometimes a soil will have a hard, compacted, impervious layer about 30 cm (12 inches) below the surface, known as a pan. It needs to be broken up to allow surface water to drain down and, more importantly, to allow the water that is held in the lower layers of the soil to rise to the surface by capillary action.

The soil should be thought of as a tank that can only hold a limited amount of water. A free-draining sandy soil will hold less water than a heavy soil. Provided that the tank is full at the start of the growing season it will be necessary to top up the tank according to the needs of the crop being grown and the amount of rain that falls. If the rainfall is low then the gardener has to resort to artificial irrigation.

Top tip

Line pea and bean trenches with newspapers to act as blotting paper and keep the root systems well supplied with moisture.

Top tip

Use the chopped-up stalks of sweetcorn in the bottom of trenches. They can hold a lot of moisture.

Artificial irrigation

Artificial irrigation is damaging to the structure of the soil. The size of the water droplets is much larger than raindrops and the amount of water applied is greater than that of a shower of rain. To quote one example: the average rainfall in the UK is 63 mm (2.5 inches) over approximately 12 days. When using artificial irrigation, 25 mm (1 inch) can be applied in a couple of hours. This is where good soil structure is important – because the impact of the large droplets can cause the soil to develop a crust or cap. Once this cap has formed any water that falls on it is prevented from entering the soil. Instead it forms puddles on the surface.

The best type of irrigation to use is in the form of a fine spray; for example, a watering can fitted with a fine rose. Overhead irrigation can be wasteful because most of the water either evaporates in the heat of the day or fails to reach the root zone because of the foliage cover of the plants. Leaky hosepipe that is manufactured from recycled car tyres is probably the best form of irrigation. This can be bought from garden centres. The pipe is laid on the surface of the soil underneath the foliage of the crop and a steady drip of water soon floods the soil.

Top tip

The most beneficial time to water plants is during the cool of the late afternoon.

Top tip

Always keep a full watering can ready to use in an emergency. It should be left in the greenhouse for a couple of hours before use to allow the water to warm up.

Watering when transplanting

To ensure the rapid establishment of transplanted crops the soil must be moist beforehand and each plant should be well watered in to at least a 150-mm (6-inch) diameter around the stem. This way no water is wasted on any unproductive ground. In hot sunny weather the plants will appreciate being watered overhead to reduce any evaporation through the leaves. Do not be tempted to drown the plants – it is a wasteful use of water.

Conservation of water

Water is becoming a very precious commodity across the world and it should be treated as such in the garden. Gone are the days when an endless supply of it could be taken for granted, freely available at the turn of a tap. Water meters will become familiar to all of us and we should all become more responsible in our use of water.

It is surprising how little water is needed in the garden if the soil is prepared in the correct way. It all starts with winter digging. This opens up the soil to soak up the rains of winter. This is then followed up with the cultivation of the soil in the spring. If possible, no more turning over of the soil should be carried out after March. All of the moisture that is trapped in the soil is lost by digging too late in the spring. Once the soil begins to warm up in the spring, a 75-mm (3-inch) deep mulch of organic material should be spread all over the surface of the soil to prevent the soil moisture being lost through evaporation. If mulching materials are in short supply, a traditional method of creating a barrier to the drying effects of the elements is a dust mulch. This is created by regular hoeing of the soil to create a fine dust-like surface about 5–7.5 cm (2–3 inches) deep that works perfectly to conserve soil water.

'One hoeing is worth two waterings.'

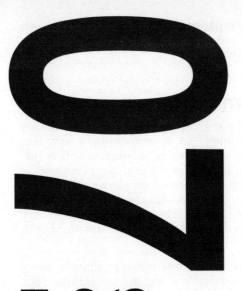

07

growing in containers and raised beds

In this chapter you will learn:
- which composts to use for container growing
- what types of containers are available
- how to construct a raised bed.

The only limitation to the range of vegetables that can be grown in containers and raised beds is the size of each crop and the amount of growing room available.

Growing medium

The best type of compost for growing vegetables in containers and raised beds is John Innes No 2. It contains a sufficient quantity of nutrients to last over three months, which is just about enough for most crops. One of the non-loam composts is an acceptable alternative, but it will need supplementary feeding after about a month to six weeks. Also, managing the watering of the non-loam compost is much more critical. They can dry out very rapidly in the summer and can become waterlogged in the winter.

It is possible to make homemade John Innes-type compost using garden soil, but it is only advisable if you are certain that your soil is free from soil-borne diseases such as club root of brassicas.

Here is a recipe for homemade soil-based compost based on the John Innes formula.

- 12 shovels of soil
- 3 shovels of peat or leaf mould
- 2 shovels of coarse/horticultural grit
- 125 gm (4 oz) general fertilizer.

Mix them well, adding the ingredients one at a time, and use the compost as soon as possible.

Containers

If you only have a small area and only containers to work with, it is best to grow the varieties of spring and summer vegetables that you particularly like or that are too expensive to buy in the shops.

The container can be made of terracotta, plastic, wood, metal or concrete – all of them are suitable, but it must be taken into account that they will all respond to heat and cold in different ways. Terracotta and wood containers will provide a buffer against the extremes of atmospheric temperatures, whereas plastic and metal will heat up violently and chill rapidly, putting the root systems of the plants under a great strain. Avoid using timber that has been treated with a wood preservative because of the risk posed by the chemical leaching out of the timber into the soil/compost, which will cause damage to the plants.

The size and depth of the container used must be suitable for the vegetables you intend to grow in it. Shallow-growing crops such as lettuces, short carrots and radishes will only require about 30 cm (12 inches) depth of soil. Deeper-rooting varieties of vegetables like French beans, maincrop carrots, cabbage, salad potatoes and tomatoes will need at least twice that depth. It is wiser to grow what are called 'baby vegetables' rather than aim to harvest full-size open-ground crops.

Top tip

Where growing space is limited grow cut and come again types of lettuce. These can be cut and allowed to re-grow several times during the course of a season.

Raised beds

Raised beds are an excellent way of growing vegetables. If you have difficulty in reaching the soil they will allow you to garden without having to bend. Make the beds about 90 cm (3 ft) tall and just wide enough so that the middle of the bed can be reached easily from both sides without having to overstretch. Leave enough working room around them to allow the use of a wheelbarrow or trolley. Do not make the beds too long. This will avoid making unnecessarily long journeys to get around them. Site the beds well away from the shade of overhanging trees and buildings and, if is possible, construct the beds to run north–south. This orientation will spread the light and warmth from the sun evenly along both sides of the plants. If you want to grow taller plants like peas and beans, plant them on the northern edge of the bed and grow the shorter crops in front of them.

Raised beds can either be made a permanent or a temporary structure in the garden. There is a range of materials that they can be constructed from. The most commonly used is pressure-treated timber boards. Bricks and concrete blocks are also a very popular choice, but they do require basic building skills to construct. Raised bed kits are also available in wood or plastic.

They are easy to put together and do not require too much in the way of site preparation beforehand.

As a general rule:

- The bottom third of the raised bed should be filled with broken bricks or coarse gravel to provide perfect drainage.

- The middle third of the raised bed should be made up from coarse organic material such as leaf mould, garden compost or well-rotted wood chips. This layer will retain moisture and ensure that the growing area never dries out.

- The top third of the raised bed is made up from ordinary garden soil or a soil-based compost such as John Innes No 2. It is best to use John Innes No 3 for stronger growing plants such as fruit trees and bushes.

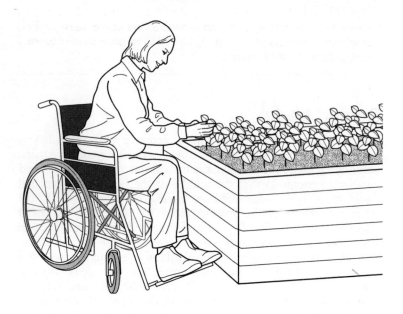

figure 7.1 raised beds

Advantages of growing in raised beds

- They allow gardeners with mobility difficulties to garden. A raised bed can be managed from a standing or sitting position.
- They are accessible from all sides.

- The soil in them warms up more quickly, allowing for earlier sowings and plantings to be made.
- They are twice as productive as the open ground.
- The weeding and pest control management is much easier.

Growing bags

The most popular method of container growing is the growing bag. These are plastic bags that are filled with a mixture of peat and fertilizer. They are perfect to use on balconies, in courtyard gardens or in the greenhouse. Growing bags are ideally suited for the cultivation of tomatoes, cucumbers, peppers and all salad crops. The bags are ready to use straight from the garden centre or garden store – all that is required is to cut an X-shaped slit in the top of the bag to plant the crop. A few holes have to be punched in the side of the bag to provide drainage. The fertilizer in the bag will only last for one month, so after this supplementary liquid feeding will have to be used weekly.

08

planning your garden

In this chapter you will learn:
- why it is important to rotate crops in the garden
- how to plan a crop rotation system
- how to get the most out of a small plot.

Whatever the size of your garden, always make a scale plan of the area. It only needs to be a rough sketch but it will let you know exactly just how much room you actually have to work with and not how much you imagine you have. A rough scale of 25 mm (1 inch) to 30 cm (12 inches) is sufficient to allow you to plan the plot. Do not forget to allow for access paths. You must be able to walk between the rows to care for the plants and to harvest them when the time comes.

Crop rotations

Plants require different nutrients from the soil and they will only use the specific nutrients that they need. However, they also excrete waste products into the soil via their roots. They can also attract specific pests that will attack and damage them, such as cabbage root fly. When plants are repeatedly grown on the same piece of ground there is the risk of attack from soil-borne pests and diseases. To prevent this happening, gardeners rotate their crops. Crop rotation is when groups of vegetables are grown on a fresh site each year, which helps to prevent the build up of pests and diseases to harmful levels. Most rotations operate on a four-year cycle, which means that a crop will only be grown on a section of the vegetable garden every fourth year. It is important to observe the rotations to keep your soil in good condition and produce first-class crops.

The table below illustrates how four crops can be rotated over four years.

Four-crop rotation

Plot	Year 1	Year 2	Year 3	Year 4
A	Legumes	Brassicas	Roots	Others
B	Brassicas	Roots	Others	Legumes
C	Roots	Others	Legumes	Brassicas
D	Others	Legumes	Brassicas	Roots

In year five the legumes return to plot A, brassicas to plot B, roots to plot C and others to plot D. The rotation cycle is then repeated for the next four years.

- Legumes are all of the members of the pea and bean family.
- Brassicas are cabbages, sprouts, broccoli, kale, radish, turnips, kohlrabi.
- Roots are all of the members of the onion and carrot families.
- Others include potatoes, beetroot, spinaches, chard, squashes, pumpkins, marrows, lettuce or any crop that does not present any serious pest or disease problems.

What size of plot do I need?

The minimum size of plot required to provide a sufficient supply of fresh produce for two adults is approximately 18 square metres or 200 square feet (6 m × 3 m/20 ft × 10 ft). The cropping plan would have to be carefully thought through to ensure that the maximum use is made of every spare piece of soil, but this is part of the fun.

Suggested cropping plan for a small plot

Intercropping, which is the growing of quicker-maturing crops in between the rows of other slower-maturing crops, is a good way of using a small space.

Suitable crops include:

- lettuces or beetroot grown in between rows of leeks, peas or broad beans
- turnips, radish or kohlrabi grown in between rows of Brussels sprouts or sprouting broccoli.

Successional cropping is when one main crop is followed with another main crop.

Suitable crops include:

- peas, broad beans, French and runner beans with all members of the brassica family
- summer cabbage with autumn-planted garlic
- Brussels sprouts with summer onions
- sprouting broccoli with maincrop carrots and leeks
- potatoes with overwintering peas and broad beans.

A suggested cropping plan for a small plot would be as follows:

Runner beans
Broad beans and leaf spinaches
Peas and lettuce
Brassicas
Leeks
Parsnips
Maincrop onions
Carrots
Beetroot
Marrows, squashes, pumpkins and courgettes
Potatoes

Cropping plan for a standard allotment

If you have a standard size allotment garden measuring approximately 9 m × 28 m (30 ft × 90 ft) an ideal cropping plan would be as follows:

MAIN CROP	SUCCESSIONAL CROP
Legumes	**Brassicas**
Broad beans	Cabbages
French beans	Brussels sprouts
Runner beans	Kales
Peas	Cauliflowers and broccoli
Brassicas	**Roots**
Spring cabbage	Onions
Brussels sprouts	Maincrop carrots and celeriac
Sprouting broccoli and kales	Leeks and Florence fennel
Winter cabbage	Parsnips and early carrots

Roots	Others
Garlic and shallots	Beetroot
Carrots and onions	Potatoes
Leeks and parsnips	Courgettes and squashes
Celeriac and Florence fennel	Leaf greens
Others	**Legumes**
Beetroot	Broad beans
Potatoes	French beans
Courgettes and squashes	Runner beans
Leaf greens	Peas

Any crop within the rotation can follow where space allows.

Top tip

Prepare a planting plan before you order your seeds and stick to it, even it if it doesn't work properly. Keep a plan of each season and record on it any changes you have made. By doing this you will eventually end up with a system that works for you.

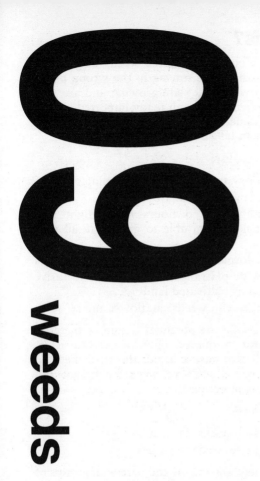

09

weeds

In this chapter you will learn:

- what methods you can use to control weeds
- what different sorts of chemical weedkillers are available
- about the need for the safe use and storage of chemicals.

What are weeds?

Many species of plant occur as unwanted weeds in gardens. Weeds are simply plants that are growing in the wrong place. They are often native to where they are growing and are well adapted to their environment (although many imported species can also be very troublesome). They can be a real problem and keeping on top of them can be a constant chore.

Weeds are so successful because:

- they have stronger root systems than the crop being grown
- they produce an abundance of seed
- many weeds are indifferent to hours of daylight and temperature, which makes them able to germinate all year round
- weed seeds can remain dormant in the soil for three to 15 years
- weeds can tolerate a wide pH range. They are able to thrive on poor ground as well as cultivated land
- through careless management, weeds can flower and set seed.

Weeds can cause a decrease in the potential weight of the crop because they compete for resources: light, water, nutrients, growing space. They will also pose a health threat to the crop because many of them are alternative hosts for fungal and bacterial disease as well as insect pests.

There are two types of weeds:

- broad leaved – groundsel, docks, fat hen
- narrow leaved – the grasses, sedges, rushes.

Within the two groups there are annual and perennial groups of plants.

Many weeds are able to increase rapidly because they have highly developed methods of seed distribution. They have windblown 'parachutes' (e.g. dandelions), explosive seed heads (e.g. bitter cress) and sticky or barbed seed coats (e.g. cleavers). Certain weeds produce several generations in the course of a season: they grow, flower and set seed in a very short period of time.

Controlling weeds

The main methods of controlling weeds are:

- physical – hoeing, hand weeding, burning, digging in
- cultural – using mulches
- chemical – using liquid or granular herbicides.

The physical method relies entirely upon:

- the removal of the weed plant from the soil
- burying it deeply enough that it decomposes in the soil
- hoeing, so that the roots and foliage are severed by the cutting action of the hoe blade and left on the surface of the soil to die. Hoeing is always best carried out on a windy or hot sunny day when the weeds will shrivel and die quickly.

Top tip

Try to hoe weeds when they are at the seedling stage; then they can be left on the surface of the soil to shrivel.

Top tip

Never leave large weeds on the surface of the soil as they still have the capacity to produce seeds. Always remove them.

Mulches have proved to be a very effective method of weed control. By placing a deep covering of organic or non-organic material on the weed-free surface of weed-free soil the weed seeds are prevented from emerging, and perennial root systems are weakened and become unable to produce too much foliage.

The chemicals or herbicides, more commonly known as weedkillers, fall into three categories:

- **Contact** herbicides kill anything containing chlorophyll (the green in leaves). They are mainly used to kill annual weeds. They may check perennial weeds but only for a short time.
- **Systemic or translocated** herbicides control a wide range of weeds. The chemical is absorbed into the plant's sap system through the leaves and is moved through the plant to the roots, where it causes gradual death over 3–4 weeks.

- **Residual** herbicides – soil acting. This type of weedkiller has to be applied to a weed-free surface and is very persistent, remaining active for up to 12 months. They function by killing any germinating seeds in the top 5–7 cm (2–3 inches) of the soil, where the chemical is absorbed by young roots. The ground must not be cultivated after application – if the soil is disturbed the seedlings will be able to emerge.

Caution!

All chemicals must be used and stored safely. Always follow the manufacturer's instructions to the letter. Be aware that children and family pets must be excluded from any treated areas for a safe period of time. Safe storage of any chemical is a legal requirement: always keep the chemicals in locked, leak-proof containers within locked buildings. Never store any mixed, unused weedkiller – always calculate how much is required to cover a given area and mix the correct quantity. It is illegal to pour any unused weedkiller, or the water/washings after cleaning out the applicators/sprayers, down drains of any description. The threat to wildlife in the garden must always be taken into consideration before using any chemicals.

10

vegetable varieties

In this chapter you will learn:
- how to grow the different families of vegetables
- what unusual and less well-known vegetables are available
- how to grow greenhouse crops
- when crops should be harvested with a month-by-month guide.

Choosing your vegetables

One of the most exciting experiences in the vegetable garden is when the first of the harvesting begins. Whether cutting a lettuce, picking broad beans or plucking juicy red tomatoes from the bush, that sense of achievement never diminishes. The problem the gardener always faces is the balancing act that is required to maintain a steady supply of produce from the garden to the kitchen all the year round. It is easy to be seduced by the glowing photographs and poetic descriptions of vegetable after vegetable in the seed catalogues. The difficulty is narrowing down the seed order to avoid the feast or famine trap that all gardeners face at some time or another. The only practical advice that can be offered here is to be prepared to listen to the more experienced gardeners around you, and to take advantage of their local knowledge of what will grow well in your locality, and more importantly, what will not.

This chapter details a selection of vegetables that will provide a wide range of fresh, healthy produce that can either be consumed straight from the garden or can be harvested at the end of summer and put into store to be used during the winter (see chart on page 113).

The names of varieties have been left out deliberately because, as already mentioned, successful cultivars (plant varieties) will vary from region to region. Also, the seed breeders and seed companies introduce new varieties every year, some of which will stand the test of time and others which will vanish from the scene quite quickly.

The vegetables described have been listed as they would be grouped together within the four-crop rotation system. To avoid constant repetition it goes without saying that the vegetable plot must be kept weed free at all times, either through regular hoeing or the use of a mulch between the rows and plants. The amount of watering that has to be carried out will depend on the crop being grown and the prevailing weather conditions.

The Latin or botanical name has been added to the more commonly used name to illustrate and help identify the individual groups within a family.

Brassicas

These are available to be freshly picked from the garden over the 12 months of the year. They form the backbone of the winter and early spring harvest. The soil for the members of the cabbage family should be fertile and well supplied with organic matter. They grow best in an alkaline soil with a pH of 7.0–7.5 When transplanting brassicas, always plant them 5 cm (2 inches) deeper than they were in the seed row.

Cabbage – *Brassica oleracea capitata*

Spring cabbage

Spring cabbages are sown in a prepared seedbed during midsummer and then transplanted to their final positions during September/October. They are hardy enough to survive the winter and are ready for harvesting from late March until May. To help them wake up from their winter rest, give the plants a top dressing of a general fertilizer such as pelleted chicken manure.

Sow from July to August, thinly in rows 12 mm (0.5 inches) deep in a prepared seedbed. Thin the seedlings to 8 cm (3 inches) apart.

Transplant to their final growing site during September and October, spacing plants at 30 cm (12 inches) in lines 30 cm (12 inches) apart.

Harvest from late March until late April.

Summer cabbage

This group of cabbages are sown during the spring to be transplanted into the open ground.

Sow from late March to April, thinly in rows 12 mm (0.5 inches) deep in a prepared seedbed. Thin the seedlings to 8 cm (3 inches) apart.

Transplant early June to their final growing site, spacing the plants at 45 cm (18 inches) in lines 45 cm (18 inches) apart.

Harvest from July until October.

Autumn and winter cabbage

The seed for these two groups of cabbage is sown during the summer in a prepared seedbed to be transplanted into their final growing positions.

Sow during May, thinly in rows 12 mm (0.5 inches) deep in a prepared seedbed. Later thin the seedlings to 8 cm (3 inches) apart.

Transplant to their final growing site during July, spacing the plants at 45 cm (18 inches) in lines 45 cm (18 inches) apart.

Harvest from November through to March.

Savoy cabbage – winter cabbage
Savoy cabbages are hardier than other winter types and are a better choice for growing on poor soils. They have wrinkled leaves that produce a squeaking sound when they are squeezed.

Sow from May to June in a prepared seedbed.

Transplant from July until August, spacing the plants at 60 cm (2 ft) in rows 60 cm (2 ft) apart.

Harvest from late November until February.

Top tip

After harvesting a cabbage cut a '+' shape into the stump to encourage four baby cabbages to re-grow.

Brussels sprouts – *Brassica oleracea gemmifera*

Brussels sprouts must be grown in firm ground to produce firm, tight sprouts. If they are grown on ground that has been dug recently and is still loose they will produce open sprouts that are known as 'blowers' and are useless.

Sow from March to April, thinly in rows 12 mm (0.5 inches) deep in a prepared seedbed. Thin the seedlings to 10 cm (4 inches) apart.

Transplant to final growing site during May to June, spacing the plants at 1 m (3 ft) in lines 1 m (3 ft) apart.

Harvest from November until March.

Aftercare: Remove the large leaves as they turn yellow, starting with the lower ones first. When picking the sprouts never cut them with a knife – they should be snapped off cleanly by pushing the sprout downwards. Always start at the bottom of the stalk and work upwards.

Broccoli – *Brassica olearacea botrytis cymosa*

Sprouting broccoli carries the winter harvest well into the spring; in a good season the broccoli will remain in production until early May. It is well worth growing for the tender, succulent young florets that cannot be beaten for flavour.

Purple and white sprouting

Sow from April to May under glass. Prick out singly into 9 cm (3.5 inch) pots to grow on before transplanting out.

Transplant from July to August, spacing plants at 75 cm (2 ft 6 inches) in lines 75 cm (2 ft 6 inches) apart.

Harvest from March through April. Cut the florets while they are still closed to maintain a steady supply.

Calabrese

This is better described as 'green sprouting broccoli'. It is milder than the traditional winter sprouting broccoli.

Sow from April to May in a prepared seedbed, later thinning the plants to 9 cm (3.5 inches) apart.

Transplant from June to July, spacing plants at 45 cm (18 inches) in lines 45 cm (18 inches) apart.

Harvest from August onwards.

Cauliflower – *Brassica olearacea botrytis*

Summer and autumn varieties

Sow the seed of the summer cultivars during January under glass, or March/April in prepared seedbeds. Sow the seed of the autumn cauliflowers in prepared seedbeds during April/May.

Transplant the summer cultivars during March to June and the autumn cultivars from late June to July. Space plants at 60 cm (2 ft) in lines 60 cm (2 ft) apart.

Harvest from June to November.

Winter varieties

Sow from April to May in open ground.

Transplant from June to July, spacing plants at 60 cm (2 ft) in lines 60 cm (2 ft) apart.

Harvest from January through May.

Kale or borecole – *Brassica oleracea acephala*

All members of the kale family are winter hardy. The kales will grow on almost any type of soil with no problems. They are surprisingly tasty and a reliable source of fresh leaves all through the winter. There are several types, curly and plain. The name borecole applies to the curly leaved cultivars.

Sow from May to June in a prepared seedbed.

Transplant from June to August, spacing plants at 60 cm (2 ft) in lines 60 cm (2 ft) apart.

Harvest from November until April.

Kohlrabi – *Brassica oleracea caulorapa*

Sometimes called the 'German turnip', this is grown for its swollen white- or purple-skinned stem that is harvested when it is the size of a golf ball.

There are two types: white and purple. The white form is the hardier and must be used for the early sowings, and the purple used for the later crops.

Sow from April to June in short rows, thinning the seedlings later. They can be transplanted, but in most cases they end up bolting.

Plant 30 cm (12 inches) apart with a distance of 30 cm (12 inches) between rows.

Harvest from July to October.

Aftercare: Water often during dry periods to prevent them from becoming woody.

Radish – *Raphanus sativus*

Radishes will grow in any well-cultivated soil. They take about six weeks from sowing to harvesting. Sow in short rows every three weeks to maintain a regular supply throughout the summer. The winter cultivars can remain in the ground until they are required for use.

Summer
Sow from late February to May – after this the temperatures are too high.

Thin to 7.5 cm (3 inches) between plants, with 23 cm (9 inches) between rows.

Harvest from April until July. Harvest while young otherwise the radish will become hot and woody.

Aftercare: Thin early to prevent overcrowding. Hoe regularly and water often in dry weather.

Winter
Sow from September to October.

Thin to 15 cm (6 inches) between plants, with 30 cm (12 inches) between rows.

Harvest from October until February. Pull the roots as they are required. Winter radish can be allowed to grow much larger than the summer types. They can sometimes become as large as turnips. Although they are winter hardy it is wise to protect them against any extreme winter weather.

Aftercare: Thin early to prevent overcrowding. Hoe regularly and water often in dry weather.

Swede – rutabaga – *Brassica napus napobrassica*

Swedes demand open, airy field conditions to grow well. They will suffer from being grown in enclosed areas. If you cannot meet their requirements, it is better to concentrate on raising turnips.

Sow from June to July at a depth of 12 mm (0.5 inches).

Thin to 23 cm (9 inches) between plants, with 45 cm (18 inches) between rows.

Harvest from October onwards.

Aftercare: Keep weed free and water well at all times.

Turnips – *Brassica rapa*

Sow in April using an early cultivar until August. Make successional sowings every three weeks, switching maincrop cultivars for the summer crop.

Plant at a depth of 12 mm (0.5 inches), with 15 cm (6 inches) between plants and 45 cm (18 inches) between rows. Thin the seedlings at the two-leaf stage.

Harvest from June until October. Pull and use as required during the summer. The later sowings can be lifted to be put into store. Select only healthy and undamaged roots and put them into boxes, covering them with dry sand or old potting compost.

Turnip tops

A late sowing of turnips can be made during August to produce fresh, young foliage. If the seed is sown thinly enough there should be no need to thin the plants. Set the rows at 30 cm (12 inches) apart.

Brassica summary

Variety	Sow	Transplant	Harvest
Spring cabbage	July/Aug	September	March–April
Summer cabbage	March/April	May	June–September
Autumn cabbage	April	May	August–October
Winter cabbage	May	July	November–February
Brussels sprouts	March/April	May/June	November–March
Sprouting Broccoli	April/May	June/July	late February–April
Green broccoli	April/May	June/July	September–October
Cauliflower – summer	October	March	July–August
Cauliflower – autumn	March/April	May	June–July
Cauliflower – winter	April/May	May/June	March–June next year
Kale	April/May	July	October–March
Kohlrabi	March/July	Sow direct	June–October
Radish – spring/ summer	Feb/July	Sow direct	April–September
Radish – winter	Aug/Sept	Sow direct	October–March
Swede	June/July	Sow direct	October–February
Turnip	Feb/Aug	Sow direct	June–December

Legumes

Legumes prefer a rich, well-drained soil with a high organic matter content, preferably dug in during the winter. If the soil has been manured, no dressings of fertilizers will be required.

All peas and beans will benefit from a top dressing of garden lime to keep the pH around 6.7 to 7.0.

Broad beans – *Vica faba*

The earliest crops can be raised from hardy (longpod) seed sown under glass during late October/early November. For small quantities of plants fill 9-cm (3.5-inch) pots with fresh potting compost and sow one seed per pot or, for larger numbers, use seed trays and sow 20 seeds per tray. Transplant the young broad bean plants into the open ground before the middle of November. These early raised beans will need to be cloched against the worst of the winter weather.

Early outdoor sowings, using the hardier longpod varieties

Plants raised under glass can be transplanted as soon as conditions permit. Make sure that the plants are hardened off before transplanting them out.

The first outdoor sowings can be made during late February as soon as the soil is in a fit condition. To maintain a continuity of supply, make further successional sowings during March and April.

Sow through February/March/April at a depth of drill 50 mm (2 inches).

Plant with 23 cm (9 inches) between plants and 30 cm (12 inches) between rows.

Harvest from late April to May.

Maincrop sowings – using the Windsor varieties. There are also dwarf strains available that are more suitable for smaller gardens and container growing.

Sow from February to April at a depth of 50 mm (2 inches).

Plant with 23 cm (9 inches) between plants and 30 cm (12 inches) between rows.

Harvest from June until August.

Aftercare: Hoe regularly around the plants and water them well when the pods begin to form. Broad beans are prone to attack from blackfly (black bean aphid): to prevent this, pinch out the soft young tips of the plants as soon as they are in full flower. Always pick the beans while they are young and tender.

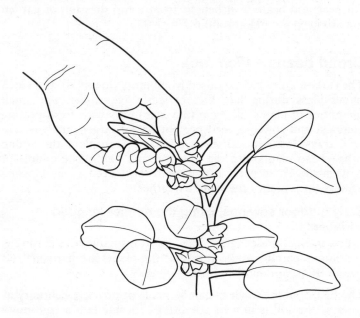

figure 10.1 pinching out growing tip

Climbing French/pole beans – *Phaseolus vulgaris*

Sow from mid-May to mid-June, 50 mm (2 inches) deep in the open ground, using the darker-skinned seed for the earliest sowings. Sow two seeds per station, removing the weaker seedling at the first true leaf stage.

Transplant outside during late May to early June if seed has been sown under glass in pots or seed trays during April. These early plantings must be protected against late frosts.

Plant 30 cm (12 inches) apart with 60 cm (2 ft) between rows. Climbing French beans can also be grown to cover a wigwam structure.

Harvest from late June until October.

Dwarf French beans – *Phaseolus vulgaris*

Sow from mid May to July, 50 mm (2 inches) deep in the open ground outdoors, using the darker-skinned seed for the earliest sowings. Sow two seeds per station, removing the weaker seedling at the first true leaf stage.

Transplant outside during late May to early June if seed has been sown under glass in pots or seed trays during April. These early plantings must be protected against late frosts.

Plant 30 cm (12 inches) apart with 60 cm (2 ft) between rows.

Harvest from July until October.

Runner beans – *Phaseolus coccineus*

Always sow the seed or plant to the left of the pole to encourage the leader to cling and climb naturally.

Sow from May to early July, 50 mm (2 inches) deep, sowing two seeds per station and removing the weaker seedling at the first true leaf stage.

Transplant outside during late May to early June if seed has been sown under glass in pots or seed trays during April. These early plantings must be protected against late frosts.

Plant 30 cm (12 inches) apart with 1 m (3 ft) between rows.

Harvest from July until October.

Aftercare: Hoe regularly and apply a mulch of organic matter before the soil's surface begins to dry out. Tie any wayward leaders to their pole and water as required. The tips of the leaders can be pinched out when the beans reach the top of their supports. Give the plants a light spraying of plain water in the cool of the evening to encourage the flowers to set. Pick the beans when they are young and tender to keep the plants cropping.

Top tip

If the flowers of runner beans are not setting (forming beans) water around the plants with limewater. Mix one handful of lime into a 10-litre (2-gallon) watering can of water.

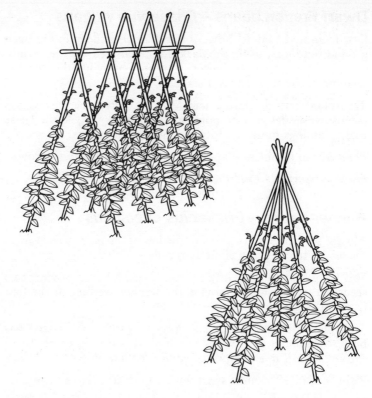

figure 10.2 runner bean supports – crossed poles and wigwam

Peas – *Pisum sativum*

Round-seeded varieties of pea seed are the hardiest types and they are used for all of the early sowings. The later and maincrop peas are known as wrinkled seeded, but these must not be sown until after mid-March.

The earliest sowings to overwinter outdoors

For these it will be beneficial to apply a dressing of potash at 15 gm (0.5 oz) per square metre/yard prior to the November sowing.

Sow in late October/November to overwinter under cloches. Use a dwarf cultivar because these plants will spend most of their growing lives under cloches.

Transplant in early November any pots or trays of peas that have been raised during October.

Depth of drill – 50 mm (2 inches).

Distance between plants – 7.5 cm (3 inches).

Distance between rows – 23 cm (9 inches).

Harvest from April to May.

Aftercare: Protect the young pea plants from the worst of the winter weather using cloches.

Early sowing outdoors using round-seeded cultivars
Sow from February to early March at a depth of 50 mm (2 inches).

Transplant during early March any earlier raised plants in pots or seed trays.

Distance between plants – 7.5 cm (3 inches).

Distance between rows – 23 cm (9 inches).

Harvest from May to June.

Maincrop using wrinkled seed cultivars
Sow from mid-March to July at a depth of 75 mm (3 inches).

Distance between plants – 7.5 cm (3 inches).

Distance between rows – 23 cm (9 inches).

Harvest from June until August.

Aftercare: Hoe regularly, keeping the ground clean between the plants. Erect pea support as soon as the plants are 7.5 cm (3 inches) tall, before they fall over and lay on the ground, otherwise they will be unable to recover and climb up the sticks or netting. The dwarf peas will not require any supporting system. Do not be tempted to over-water the plants in the early stages but be prepared to water frequently after flowering commences to encourage well-filled pods.

Other kinds of peas
These are grown in exactly the same way as garden peas except the pea pods are eaten and not the pea.

Sugar snap peas are plump little pods that are fit for eating when the pods snap cleanly in two. They may be cooked or eaten raw.

Mangetout are eaten as thin, flat, succulent pea-less pods, best eaten when cooked for a short while.

> **Top tip**
> Pinch out the tops of pea plants as soon as the flowers are open. This will speed up the filling of the pod.

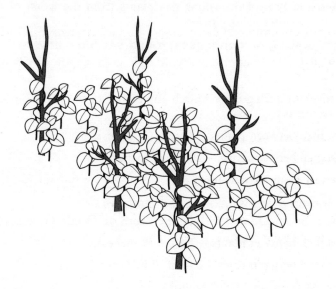

figure 10.3 pea sticking

Roots – carrot family

Carrots, parsnips, celeriac, celery and Florence fennel require a deep fertile soil. They do not like freshly manured ground. They are best grown following other crops that have previously been grown in manured soil. Avoid stony ground as this will cause the roots to fork and become misshapen. Leave the soil rough throughout winter until sowing time before preparing a fine tilth.

A pH of 6.5–7.5 is best. Early crops should be grown on lighter soil; the main crops will tolerate slightly heavier soils.

Carrots – *Daucus carota*

Earliest sowings under glass, cloches or frames
Sow from November to February.

Depth of drill – 18 mm (0.75 inches).

Distance between plants – 7.5 cm (3 inches).

Distance between rows – 30 cm (12 inches).

Harvest from April to July.

Earliest sowings outdoors using quick maturing cultivars
Sow in March and early April.

Depth of drill – 18 mm (0.75 inches).

Distance between plants – 7.5 cm (3 inches).

Distance between rows – 30 cm (12 inches).

Harvest from late May to June.

Maincrop
Carrots grown from seed sown after June do not suffer from attack by carrot root fly.

Sow from June to July in open ground.

Depth of drill – 18 mm (0.75 inches).

Distance between plants – 10 cm (4 inches).

Distance between rows – 30 cm (12 inches).

Harvest from August to October.

Aftercare
Hoe between the rows and thin the seedlings when the rough leaves are produced. Later thinnings can be used in the kitchen. To reduce the threat of attack from carrot root fly only thin on cool, dull days or late in the afternoon. Always water along the rows to settle the plants back in after thinning.

Top tip

Water carrots regularly to avoid them developing split or forked roots.

Harvesting and storing

Pull the early carrots as soon as they are large enough to be used. The maincrop carrots that are intended for storing are lifted in October and put into clamps or boxes and covered with damp sand. In milder regions the last-sown crops can be left in the soil until required, although they may have to be protected from frosty conditions with a layer of straw.

Parsnips – *Pastinaca sativa*

Parsnip seed can take up to three weeks to germinate. Sow at the earliest opportunity from March onwards. Delay sowing seed if the weather and soil conditions are cold and wet. It is better to wait a little longer rather than allow the seed to rot in the soil, otherwise precious time will have been wasted waiting in vain for the seedlings to emerge.

Sow from March to May. Parsnip seed has a short shelf life. Always use new, fresh seed every year to avoid disappointment. Sow thinly, or space two or three seeds at 15 cm (6 inches) apart. Thin carefully at the first true leaf stage to one seedling per station; water along the row to settle the seedling back in. Finally thin to 30 cm (12 inches) to grow on.

Depth of drill – 18 mm (0.75 inches).

Distance between plants – 30 cm (12 inches).

Distance between rows – 45 cm (18 inches).

Harvest from November to March.

Aftercare

Wait until the parsnips have been frosted before lifting them; this will improve their flavour. Parsnips are perfectly frost hardy and can remain in the ground until they are required for use. If there is a danger of the ground being frozen for a period of time, lift a few roots and store them in a bucket or large pot filled with soil or old potting compost. Lift the last of the roots during March and store them somewhere cool and shady to prevent them breaking into growth.

Hamburg parsley – *Petroselinum crispum tuberosum*

Hamburg parsley is grown for its white parsnip-like root.

Sow from March to April. Hamburg parsley does not transplant successfully. The seedlings have to be thinned in the row.

Depth of drill – 12 mm (0.5 inches).

Distance between plants – 30 cm (12 inches).

Distance between rows – 30 cm (12 inches).

Harvest from late summer onwards. The plants are winter hardy and can be left in the ground and lifted as required.

Celeriac – *Apium graveolens rapaceum*

Celeriac is sometimes referred to as the German turnip-rooted celery. Celeriac produces a large swollen root that develops just above the surface of the soil. It tastes just like celery but is much easier to grow. It is a hardy vegetable and is able to withstand a couple of degrees of frost. It can be used during the winter if it is lifted before the worst of the cold weather arrives and stored in boxes of damp sand or old potting compost. It can be eaten raw or used in soups or with fish dishes.

Sow from March, in seed trays under glass. Prick out into trays or 7.5-cm (3-inch) pots to grow on before planting out.

Transplant from May to June.

Distance between plants – 30 cm (12 inches).

Distance between rows – 45 cm (18 inches).

Harvest during October and November from open ground, or December and February out of store.

Aftercare
Hoe regularly between the plants. Celeriac must be watered frequently, especially during dry periods. Remove any side shoots that appear around the sides of the plants to help them develop a large swollen root.

Celery – *Apium graveolens*

Celery is a very demanding crop to grow. Like celeriac, it is descended from bog plants. Traditionally it is grown in a trench that has to be well prepared in advance. The trench is usually 45 cm (18 inches) wide by 30 cm (12 inches) deep. The bottom of the trench has to have plenty of manure or compost dug into it to increase its water-holding capacity. If the bottom of the trench is made up of poor subsoil, remove at least 20 cm (8 inches) depth of the subsoil and replace it with fertile topsoil. The trench can be left open until just before planting time to soak up the rains. Apply a dressing of pelleted chicken manure to the bottom of the trench before filling it in. Backfill the trench to within 7.5 cm (3 inches) of the top to create a reservoir to hold water. This will gradually be filled as the season progresses.

Sow from March in seed trays under glass, lightly covering the seed. When they are large enough to handle, prick out the seedlings into trays or 9-cm (3.5-inch) pots to grow on before planting out.

Transplant from late May to June, giving the plants lots of water.

Distance between plants – 30 cm (12 inches).

Distance between rows/trenches – 1.5 m (4 ft).

Harvest from October to February.

Aftercare

Water regularly to maintain steady growth, especially if the weather is dry. When the plants are around 30 cm (12 inches) it is time to carry out the first earthing up. Before doing this, remove any side shoots that appear around the base of the celery plants and then tie up the stems below the foliage. Ensure that the soil is moist before beginning to draw it around the sides of the plant. Make the first earthing up into a shallow ridge around 7.5 cm (3 inches) high; carry on, gradually increasing the height of the ridge two or three times more over the next few weeks. The final height of the ridge should be just below the point where the stalks finish and the foliage begins. Care must be taken during the earthing-up stage not to spill any soil in to the heart of the plant.

To harvest, break open the soil ridge just enough to remove a plant. Cut the root just below the base of the stems and wash the plant out thoroughly before taking to the kitchen. White forms of celery are not reliably frost hardy and have to be stored in boxes; the red stemmed celery is considered to be more frost tolerant.

Self-blanching celery

This is a type of celery that does not require the elaborate soil preparation described for trench celery. It is raised in exactly the same way as trench celery but is planted out in blocks on the surface of the soil. No earthing up is required as the plants are all shading each other. The outside ones will be less blanched than the inner plants but they will still be acceptable. Plant 23 cm (9 inches) each way in the block

Florence fennel – *Foeniculum vulgare dulce*

Florence fennel is grown for its swollen edible leaf base. It should not to be confused with the herb fennel. It requires a warm, sunny, open site with free-draining soil. The swollen leaf base has an aniseed flavour and may be eaten raw in salads or cooked either in soups or fish dishes.

Sow from May to June. Avoid sowing during very hot weather. Florence fennel will not transplant successfully. It must be sown directly in the soil and the seedlings thinned later.

Depth of drill – 12 mm (0.5 inches).

Distance between plants – 30 cm (12 inches).

Distance between rows – 30 cm (12 inches).

Harvest from September until early November.

Aftercare

Water the plants liberally to encourage leaf growth and to prevent them from bolting. Once the leaf bases begin to swell they have to be blanched. To do this the soil is drawn up just enough to completely cover the base, leaving the foliage exposed. Harvest as required for use, but Florence fennel is not reliably frost hardy so any left over at the end of summer must be lifted and stored in boxes filled with damp sand. It will only store for a short time.

Roots – onion family

The onion family comprises garlic, leeks, onions, spring onions, chives and shallots.

Garlic – *Allium sativum*

Garlic will do well in most soils but it does best in a light, free-draining soil. Always buy garlic bulbs from reputable suppliers, never be tempted to use garlic bulbs bought at supermarkets or from greengrocers. They are cultivars that have been grown out under field conditions and could be carrying diseases that will be harmful to all of the members of the onion family.

There are two types of garlic: the softneck and the hardneck. The softneck types have a longer storage life than the hardneck. The softneck is distinguished by having a soft papery stem at the top of the bulb; the hardneck produces a hard floral spike. This flower head should be removed to encourage a larger bulb. The softneck garlic does not develop a flowering stalk and produces bulbs with more but smaller cloves than the hardnecks. The hardnecks are considered to have the truer garlic flavour.

Try to plant garlic as soon as possible after the bulbs are delivered. Do not break up the whole garlic bulb until you are ready to plant out the individual cloves. There are usually eight to ten cloves in a bulb.

Winter
Plant in October and November, avoiding cold and wet soil conditions.

Spring
Plant in February and March as the soil begins to warm up. Plant at a depth of 5 cm (2 inches), making sure that the tip of the clove is just below the surface of the soil.

Distance between plants – 30 cm (12 inches).

Distance between rows – 30 cm (12 inches).

Harvest from June to July when about 50 per cent of the foliage begins to yellow and shrivel. After lifting the bulbs, dry them off in the sun for a few days or, if conditions are wet, dry them in the greenhouse before putting into storage somewhere clean and frost free. Remove any soil and loose skins before setting the bulbs out in trays. They will keep in store for up to ten months.

Aftercare: Hoe regularly between the plants. There is no need to water garlic except in severe drought conditions. Withholding water improves the quality of the crop.

Leeks – *Allium ampeloprasum porrum*

These are one of the hardiest winter vegetables to be found in the kitchen garden. They can survive freezing temperatures to last well into the spring. They appreciate a well-dug soil containing plenty of organic matter.

Sow from February in trays under glass or March in a prepared seedbed outdoors. Take care not to sow too thickly to prevent producing crowded weak plants that may bolt after transplanting. Plant at a depth of 12 mm (0.5 inches).

Transplant from May to June when the leek plants are around 15 cm (6 inches) tall, using a dibber to create 23-cm (9-inch) deep holes in which to drop the plants. Settle the young transplants into the hole using a watering can to carefully direct the water into the hole.

Distance between plants – 30 cm (12 inches).

Distance between rows – 30 cm (12 inches).

Harvest from November to March.

Aftercare: Hoe between the plants regularly, taking care not to push soil into the holes, and water frequently during dry periods. As the leeks develop they will begin to fill the holes – at this stage, draw a little soil up around the stem to increase the area of blanching.

Onions – *Allium cepa*

Onions benefit from a soil that has been well prepared. It should have been left rough-dug through the winter and the lumps knocked down and raked to a fine tilth during February. The onion bed must be made firm by treading it lightly.

Maincrop onions – early seed sowing under glass

The early sown onions will produce the largest bulbs. Onions benefit from a long growing season; the more sets of leaves that are produced before the longest day of the year the larger the onion bulb will be.

Sow from December to January. Sow the seed in trays or pots filled with seed-sowing compost under glass at a temperature of 16°C (60°F). Prick out the seedlings as soon as they begin to straighten and transplant singly into 9-cm (3.5-inch) pots or standard trays filled with potting compost, setting the seedlings 5 cm (2 inches) apart. Grow on steadily at a slightly cooler temperature until the plants are ready to transplant into the open ground during late March/April. Take care to harden the plants off before planting out.

Maincrop onions – seed sown outdoors

Sow from late March to April, as soon as soil conditions are suitable. Sow the seed thinly in the row at a depth of 12 mm

(0.5 inches). Thin to 10 cm (4 inches) apart when the plants are 5 cm (2 inches) high and water along the row to settle plants in. Thin twice more to final 30-cm (12-inch) spacing, using the thinnings as spring onions.

Distance between plants – 30 cm (12 inches).

Distance between rows – 30 cm (12 inches).

Harvest from August to September.

Maincrop onions from sets

Onion sets are small dormant onion bulbs that take all of the risk out of onion growing. They remove the threat of attack by onion root fly that is the scourge of outdoor-sown seed-raised onions after they have been transplanted.

Plant from March to April. Plant with the tip of the set just showing above the surface of the soil.

Distance between plants – 25 cm (10 inches).

Distance between rows – 30 cm (12 inches).

Harvest from August to September.

Overwintering onions from seed

These are grown to supply the gardener with the earliest onions. They are lifted to be used immediately, well before the maincrop onions are harvested.

Sow in August at a depth of 12 mm (0.5 inches) and transplant in March.

Distance between plants – 30 cm (12 inches).

Distance between rows – 30 cm (12 inches).

Harvest in June and July.

Japanese onions grown from sets

These have gained in popularity over the years. They are hardy enough to survive the winter and then provide an early summer crop of onions. Japanese onions have replaced overwintering seed-raised onions.

Sow in August. Plant with the tip of the bulb just above the surface of the soil.

Distance between plants – 20 cm (8 inches).

Distance between rows – 30 cm (12 inches).

Harvest in June.

> **Top tip**
> To prevent onions from bolting (producing a flower stalk) avoid planting them in cold wet soil.

Aftercare for all onions
Onions produce shallow root systems. Hoe lightly between the rows and hand weed around the plants. Water regularly during dry periods to prevent attack from mildew.

Harvesting
Onions become ready for harvesting from mid-August onwards. The first indication is when the foliage of the onions begins to yellow and starts to fall over. Some authorities advise bending the tops down to induce the ripening process, but this can lead to neck rots being set off. Letting the foliage fall naturally is much safer. At this stage, push a garden fork underneath the base of the bulb and gently ease the plant upwards to sever the roots and hasten the ripening process. A week or so later, lift the bulbs completely out of the ground and spread them out on the surface of the soil to dry. Lay the onions out with the basal root plate facing south or west towards the sun to completely dry the bulb.

Once the leaf growth has become like straw it can be pulled away from the bulb, severing just above the top of the neck of the onion. Either string the onions together or set them out in trays to store somewhere light and frost free until they are needed for use. Use the largest bulbs and the ones with thick necks first because they will not keep in store for very long.

Spring/pickling onions

Overwintering types
Sow from September to October.

Harvest from March to April, pulling the green onions when required for use.

Summer types
Sow from March to September, at a depth of 12 mm (0.5 inches). Sow thinly, in rows 30 cm (12 inches) apart; no thinning is required.

Harvest from May to October, pulling the green onions when required for use.

Shallots – *Allium ascalonicum*

Shallots appreciate a long growing season to produce a decent crop. It is always advised to plant shallots on the shortest day to harvest them on the longest day. This little piece of gardeners' lore is not really very practical or accurate. Wait until the middle of February to plant, when the soil is beginning to dry out and becomes more workable.

The shallot is a perennial form of the onion, so when one bulb is planted it produces six to eight offsets during the summer.

Plant in February. Always use a trowel, leaving the tip of the bulb just showing above the surface of the soil. The birds love to pull the bulbs out of the soil, leaving them on the ground. To help prevent this from happening, cut off any dried foliage that may still be attached to the bulb before planting out.

Distance between plants – 30 cm (12 inches).

Distance between rows – 30 cm (12 inches).

Harvest from June to July.

Aftercare

By the end of July the foliage will have turned straw like, and the clusters of bulbs will be ready for lifting. Gently ease them out of the ground using a garden fork and leave the bulbs on the surface of the soil to dry. If the conditions are damp, place the shallots under a cloche, in a frame or in the greenhouse to ripen before being put into store. Shallots will store well into the new year. They will have to be inspected regularly to remove any soft or decaying bulbs. Save enough healthy shallot bulbs about 25 mm (1 inch) in diameter to plant out the following season.

Shallots grown from seed

It is possible to grow shallots from seed that is sown during March in just the same way as onions. The bulbs produced from seed-sown cultivars must be used in the autumn/winter. Do not save any bulbs from these shallots to replant in the new year. The shallot is a biennial, and because of this the bulbs will produce a flower spike. Fresh seed will have to be sown every year if you wish to continue with growing the seed types.

Others

These are the varieties of vegetables that will fit safely into the rotation system without causing any pest or disease problems to other crops.

Lettuce – *Lactuca sativa*

Lettuce requires an open situation and must be grown in a fertile, well-drained soil. Apply a dressing of general fertilizer when preparing the seedbed. It is possible to harvest lettuce all the year round if you select a suitable variety.

Spring harvesting lettuce

Grown from winter-hardy lettuce varieties that are sown towards the end of summer. These plants will remain in their permanent rows during the winter and are given a top dressing of general fertilizer to boost growth in the spring.

Sow in September and October in shallow drills. Do not transplant. Thin during October to 15 cm (6 inches) as soon as the seedlings are large enough to handle. Thin again during March.

Distance between plants – 30 cm (12 inches).

Distance between rows – 30 cm (12 inches).

Harvest from March until May.

Raising early outdoor lettuces under glass

Sow in February in seed trays and pots in a propagator set to 13°C (55°F). Avoid using higher temperatures which will cause the germination to be poor. Prick out into 9-cm (3.5-inch) pots to grow on.

Transplant under cloches, during March after hardening the plants off.

Harvest from April until June.

Summer harvesting lettuce

Make fresh sowings every 21 days to maintain a continuous supply for all of the summer. Sow in short rows to avoid producing too many lettuces. Do not transplant seedlings after April because they will run to seed in hot, dry conditions.

Sow from March until July in shallow drills. Thin in the row to 30 cm (12 inches). Use thinnings to fill any gaps in the rows.

Distance between plants – 30 cm (12 inches).

Distance between rows – 30 cm (12 inches).

Harvest from June until October.

Winter lettuce

This crop is raised from seed that is sown in the late summer and then grown on under protection. There is a range of suitable forcing varieties that have been bred specially to be grown under glass. The seed is sown in a prepared seedbed and grown on in the usual way. The plants are covered with cloches or grown in glasshouses or frames to survive the worst of the winter conditions. Give plenty of ventilation on sunny days.

Sow in August in shallow drills. Thin in the row – do not transplant.

Distance between plants – 30 cm (12 inches).

Distance between rows – 30 cm (12 inches).

Harvest from November until December.

Top tip

Lettuce seed will not germinate during periods of high temperatures. After sowing the seed cover over the line of the drill with a 25-mm (1-inch) deep layer of grass clippings or used potting compost to keep the soil cool.

Top tip

Sow a fresh batch of lettuce seed every ten days to maintain a regular supply.

Chicory (*Chicorum intybus*), endive (*Chicorum endiva*) and radicchio (*Chicorum intybus*)

There is a great deal of confusion over the naming of these plants. Basically they are all of the same family, but during their cultivation they have somehow acquired separate identities. In the United Kingdom radicchio is the name used to specifically identify the red and variegated leaf types.

Chicory is known to the French as endive and to the Italians as 'endiva'. The difference between the two is that chicory is treated as a perennial and endive as a biennial. All three are cultivated in the same way. Sow the seed according to the variety.

The following vegetables benefit from being blanched before use.

Witloof chicory – *Chicorum intybus*
Witloof chicory is grown for its blanched shoots or chicons that are forced during the winter months. It is totally winter hardy and can be blanched in situ or by the more traditional method, in complete darkness in a shed or under the greenhouse staging.

Sow from May to July in open ground at a depth of 12 mm (0.5 inches).

Distance between plants – 30 cm (12 inches), thinning seedlings at the three-leaf stage.

Distance between rows – 30 cm (12 inches).

Lift roots in late October/early November.

Blanch from November to March. Only blanch enough roots for your immediate needs.

Aftercare: Witloof chicory produces a mass of green leaves that are too tough to eat. At the end of the season all the foliage is cut off just above soil level. The discarded leaves can go to the compost heap. The large roots of the plants are dug up and have to be trimmed to around 15 cm (6 inches) before being stored in boxes and covered with moist sand. When the roots are required for forcing they are set up in small batches using large flowerpots filled with sand, old compost or garden soil. Leave 25 mm (1 inch) of the top of the root protruding above the soil. Place a pot of the same size on top of the pot containing the roots and cover the drainage hole to exclude light. Place the pot in a frost-free shed or outbuilding and in four to five weeks the root will have produced a blanched shoot that is ready for the table. To maintain a steady supply, set up the roots for blanching at regular intervals.

Sugar loaf chicory – *Chicorum intybus*
Sugar loaf chicory is self-blanching – unlike Witloof chicory it does not need to be covered to produce a white heart. It looks

very much like a large cos lettuce. It produces a tight head of curled leaves that surround the heart of the plant. Unlike Witloof chicory the plants can remain in the soil until wanted, but they will require some form of protection against the worst of the weather. This could be a cloche or straw stacked over the plants. To prepare the plants for the kitchen, remove just enough of the outer leaves to reveal the blanched white heart of the plant.

Sow from June to July. Sugar loaf chicory does not transplant well. Thin the seedlings in the row.

Distance between plants – 30 cm (12 inches).

Distance between rows – 45 cm (18 inches).

Harvest from October to November. Sugar loaf is mildly frost hardy but the lower temperatures will cause the outside leaves to rot.

Endive – *Chicorum endiva*

Endive needs to be blanched before using to remove its bitter taste. It can be eaten raw or cooked and is a useful alternative to lettuce. There are two types of endive available, the curled for summer use and the Batavian or round-leaf form for late autumn and winter use.

Endive does not transplant successfully; it is better to sow the seed directly in the open ground and thin to the final spacings.

Summer

Sow from April to August at a depth of 12 mm (0.5 inches).

Distance between plants – 30 cm (12 inches).

Distance between rows – 30 cm (12 inches).

Harvest from August to February.

Late autumn/winter

Sow from August to early September directly into the soil.

Distance between plants – 45 cm (18 inches).

Distance between rows – 45 cm (18 inches).

Aftercare: The endive plants will have to be blanched a short time before the intended harvesting date. It is important to ensure that the leaves of the endive are thoroughly dry before beginning the blanching process. The plants can be covered with a flowerpot, covering the drainage hole or placing a plate or piece of slate on the top of the plant to exclude the light. Another method is to tie up a small number of leaves at a time to prevent setting up rots in the heart of the plant.

Beetroot – *Beta vulgaris*

Avoid growing beetroot in freshly manured soil. Apply a dressing of general fertilizer when preparing the seedbed.

Early cultivars

These are to harvest and use immediately.

Sow from March until May in shallow drills. The earliest sowings may need the protection of cloches or fleece.

Distance between plants – 25 cm (10 inches).

Distance between rows – 45 cm (18 inches).

Harvest from May until September.

Maincrop

These are to use and to be stored for use throughout the winter months.

Sow from July in shallow drills.

Distance between plants – 25 cm (10 inches).

Distance between rows – 45 cm (18 inches).

Harvest from September until October. The late harvest must be lifted before the first hard frosts arrive.

Aftercare: Thin seedlings to 11 cm (4.5 inches) at the first rough leaf stage and later to 22 cm (9 inches). Thin to one plant at each station.

Harvesting and storing

Pull and use the early sowings as soon as they are as large as a golf ball. The maincrop sowings that are intended to be stored are lifted in October. Only select healthy and undamaged roots to put into store. They can be stored in an earth clamp or in boxes and covered with damp sand. Beetroot will become woody if it is allowed to be frosted. Never cut the foliage off; always twist the tops off to prevent them from 'bleeding'.

Leaf vegetables

The following are all leaf crops.

Spinach

Summer – round seeded – *Spinacea oleracea inermis*

Sow from March to May.

Harvest from late May until July.

Winter – prickly seeded varieties – *Spinacea oleracea*

Sow in August at a depth of 18 mm (0.75 inches). If the prickly seeded cultivars are sown too early they will bolt and quickly run to seed.

Distance between plants – 30 cm (12 inches).

Distance between rows – 60 cm (2 ft).

Harvest from May to March.

Spinach beet – perpetual spinach – *Beta vulgaris cicla*

Drought tolerant, this does not run to seed during dry conditions.

Sow in March and August at a depth of 18 mm (0.75 inches).

Distance between plants – 30 cm (12 inches).

Distance between rows – 60 cm (2 ft).

Harvest from June through until April.

Aftercare: Cut the leaves when they are small. Pick quite often to prevent the leaves becoming coarse and tough.

Swiss chard – leaf beet – *Beta vulgaris cicla*

Swiss chard is grown for its leaves. Although it is a member of the beetroot family it does not produce an edible root. It makes a most colourful addition to the garden because there are red-, yellow- and orange-leafed cultivars as well as the more traditional green leaf types.

Sow from April to August at a depth of 25 mm (1 inch).

Distance between plants – 45 cm (18 inches).

Distance between rows – 45 cm (18 inches).

Harvest from July until October.

Aftercare: Water frequently in dry periods to keep up the leaf production and prevent the plants from running to seed. Swiss chard is tough enough to survive the winter and will produce an early crop of leaves, but it will run to seed as soon as the temperatures begin to rise.

Salsify – *Tragopogon porrifolius*

Sometimes called the vegetable oyster because its flavour is supposed to resemble that of oysters. This is a slightly exaggerated claim but still well worth growing for its delicate flavour.

Sow in April directly into drills 12 mm (0.5 inches) deep and thin later.

Distance between plants – 30 cm (12 inches).

Distance between rows – 30 cm (12 inches).

Harvest from late summer onwards. The white tapering roots are frost hardy and can be left in the ground until they are wanted for the table. They can be lifted and stored in boxes and covered with sand.

Scorzonera – *Scorzonera hispanica* is identical to salsify except it has a black skin. It requires exactly the same cultivation.

Sweetcorn – *Zea maya*

Sow during April/May under glass, or May/June outdoors under cloches.

Transplant in May/June when the threat of any late frosts has passed. Always plant sweetcorn in blocks to ensure pollination: it is a member of the grass family and is wind pollinated. By using the block system the pollen can move from plant to plant easily.

Distance between plants – 60 cm to 1 metre (2 ft to 3 ft), depending on the eventual height of the plant.

Top tip

Earth up soil around the stems of sweetcorn plants to help provide extra support.

Harvest from July until late September.

Aftercare: The cobs are ready for harvesting after the tassels on the ends of the husk have turned black. At this stage, gently peel back a little of the husk to reveal a few of the seeds. Press your thumbnail into the plump corn seed; if a milky substance squirts out the cob is ready for picking. If no milky juice is seen, wait a few more days. To remove the cob, ease it downwards so that it snaps off with a clean break. After harvesting, the cob can be kept for three or four days in the salad compartment of a refrigerator.

Supersweet varieties

Sweetcorn is notorious for losing its sweetness very quickly and developing a bland starchy flavour. To compensate for this a range of extra sweet hybrids have been developed, these are known as the supersweet hybrids. The cobs contain a much higher sugar content at the time of harvesting and they lose their sweetness gradually over many weeks. This makes them a much more attractive proposition to grow than the non-supersweet cultivars. Never grow the supersweet and other types of sweetcorn together. They will cross-pollinate and the quality of the supersweets will be damaged as a result.

The cucumber family – *Cucumis sativus*

Outdoor or ridge cucumbers

These cucumbers are far less demanding to grow than their greenhouse cousins. There are two types to choose from, the long smooth-skinned cultivars and the shorter rough-skinned forms that resemble gherkins. The young cucumber plants can either be trained up a vertical wire support or allowed to trail over the ground. If you are growing the plants against a supporting structure, the tip of the plants must be removed when they reach the top of it. Ridge cucumbers get their name from the manner in which they are grown. All members of the cucumber family require free-draining soil, and to ensure this the soil has to be drawn up to form a mound or ridge.

Sow in April under glass or May/June outdoors. The seed sown under glass during April will produce small plants that are transplanted in late May. Once the threat of frost has gone the seed can be sown directly in the open ground. It is best to use a cloche to warm the soil first and to cover the seedlings with until the plants are well established. Sow two or three seeds 18 mm (0.75 inches) deep, later thinning to the strongest seedling after the first true leaves are produced.

Transplant in late May at a distance of 1 metre (3 ft) apart. If you are using a supporting structure, the plants can be spaced out at 45-cm (18-inch) intervals along it. Space the rows by 1 metre (3 ft).

Harvest from June until September.

Aftercare: Always water well in dry weather and spray the plants overhead occasionally to prevent attacks from red spider mites. Give the plants a liquid feed once a week. Cut the plants while they are still young to maintain production.

Top tip

Cut cucumbers while they are a dark green colour. Place them on a saucer containing 12 mm (0.5 inches) of water. Store them in a cool shady room or cellar until they are required.

Frame cucumbers

These are a range of cucumbers that benefit from the extra protection of the garden frame. They allow you to produce cucumbers of a similar quality to the greenhouse types. To make the best use of the limited space that a frame offers, the fruits are about 15 cm (6 inches) in length, which is about half the size of greenhouse cucumbers. The young plants are produced and transplanted in the same way as the ridge cucumbers described above. Water the plants in and keep the frame closed up for two or three days. Cover the frame with hessian sacking or similar to prevent the temperatures inside from getting too high. Pinch out the tip of the lead shoot when four leaves have been produced. This will encourage four side shoots to develop and these must be stopped when they reach the sides of the frame.

Courgettes or zucchini – *Cucurbita pepo*

Courgettes and zucchini are the same thing. They are bush marrows and, as such, they are perfectly suited for growing in small gardens and containers. The main difference between courgettes and marrows/squashes is that the fruits of courgettes have been developed to be eaten when they are small – no longer than 15 cm (6 inches).

Sow in April under glass or during May outdoors under protection. In colder areas it is probably safer to use pot-raised plants rather than risk sowing seed in the open ground. Use the same method as described for outdoor cucumbers.

Transplant from May to June after all the threat from late frosts has passed. Plant 1 metre (3 ft) apart, with 1 metre (3 ft) between rows. Keep a cloche handy to cover the young plants if the night temperatures become low. All members of the marrow/squash family are susceptible to a stem rot if the stems of young transplants are allowed to become over-wet. To avoid this, dig out a hole about 1 metre (3 ft) in diameter when preparing the planting site, almost fill the hole with well rotted organic material and cover with the excavated soil to create a mound. Plant on the top of the mound to ensure that any excess water will drain away.

Harvest from July until September/early October. Courgettes/zucchini will not store as well as marrows and squashes. The combination of colder weather and shortening days will bring their season to an end. Lift and compost the foliage before it becomes diseased.

Marrows, pumpkins and squashes – *Cucurbita pepo* and *pepo ovifera*

Marrows, pumpkins and squashes are the same type of plant; they are all members of the same family as courgettes, but the winter squashes are classified as *Cucurbita maxima*. The summer cultivars usually have a trailing habit and the winter types are usually bushy plants.

Sow from April under glass or May outdoors.

Transplant from May to June, 1.5 m (4.5 ft) apart for the bush types and 2 metres (6 ft) for the trailing cultivars, with the same distance between rows.

Harvest from July until October. The later harvest fruits can be kept in store for at least three months. Take care to clear the patch before the first of the autumn frosts can do any damage to the crop. Store the harvested fruits somewhere dry and frost free.

Top tip

If you want to make marrows all keep pace with each other in size cut a V-shaped notch into the stems of the faster-growing ones to slow them down.

> **Top tip**
>
> Acorn and butternut squashes have the best taste but will only keep for up to eight weeks. Delay harvesting them until just before the first frost is expected.

Potatoes – *Solanum tuberosum*

Potatoes will grow in a wide range of soils, though a deep, fertile, well-drained soil with a pH of 5.0–6.0 is best. No lime should be added because it encourages potato scab. To obtain the best yields, dig in plenty of compost or manure during the autumn.

Potatoes are a very labour-intensive crop. They need to be earthed up regularly to help develop the young potatoes, and the harvesting can take several hours. They are also a bulky crop to store. It is worth considering these requirements before committing too much of the garden to potato production.

Site – potatoes enjoy full sun, so plant on an open site free from shade.

Seed – the ideal seed potato should sit in the palm of the hand quite comfortably; it should be no larger than a small hen's egg.

Chitting – this is the term used to describe the setting up of the seed potato in a tray or box to produce short green sprouts. All potatoes have a rose end, which is easily distinguished by the appearance of short young shoots known as 'eyes'. The eyes will eventually develop into shoots

Early varieties (earlies)
Plant in March. Plant tubers 30 cm (12 inches) apart at 15 cm (6 inches) depth, with a distance of 75 cm (2.5 ft) between rows.

Harvest from July onwards.

Maincrop varieties
Plant in April. Plant tubers 45 cm (18 inches) apart at 15 cm (6 inches) depth, with a distance of 75 cm (2.5 ft) between rows.

Harvest from September to October by lifting them out of the earth with a fork. Put the maincrop varieties into store for the winter months. Only save perfect disease-free potatoes for putting into store. Always use any damaged tubers first.

Storing potatoes

When potatoes are exposed to the daylight for too long they turn green and become poisonous. To prevent this happening they must be stored in complete darkness. They can be put into hessian or paper potato sacks and then stored in a building that is cool but frost free. Another traditional method of storage is the potato or root clamp. This is formed by placing a layer of straw on the soil and then setting the potatoes out in rows on the straw. More potatoes are added to the stack to form a gentle mound. Do not make the clamp more than 90 cm (3 ft) high. Line the outside of the mound with a layer of straw 'thatch' and then cover the thatch with a layer of soil. Create a straw chimney to allow the clamp to breathe and the potatoes will remain in good condition all winter until required for use.

Oriental vegetables

The term 'Oriental vegetables' covers a broad range of plants that are from a wide geographical area that includes China, Japan, Korea, Vietnam and Taiwan. It has taken the West a long time to discover these vegetables, although some of them were already being cultivated in European vegetable gardens during the 1800s, such as the *Hinonona-kabu* turnip. But they have really only grown in popularity since the 1960s and the range of varieties available to us is increasing year after year. Many of the Oriental vegetables are well suited to growing in cooler conditions and this is what makes them an ideal addition to the winter vegetable garden.

These vegetables originate from countries that had large populations to feed and only a limited amount of land available to them on which to grow crops. Strains were selected from wild vegetables that grew very quickly, so allowing them several harvests a season. Also, most importantly, they were packed with healthy goodness. Oriental vegetables are in the main leaf, stem and shoot crops that are steamed or used in stir-fry cooking, although there are a few roots and tubers too.

The Oriental vegetables are divided up into various family groups, all of which are familiar to us in our own gardens and the cultivation of which is not too difficult for us to understand.

Brassicas

This group contains the most diverse range of vegetables and includes Chinese cabbage, pak choi, broccoli shoots, leafy mizuna and mustard greens. This range of leafy brassicas grows much more quickly than some of the more traditional cauliflowers, cabbages and Brussels sprouts.

Beans

The main constituents of this group are the Japanese Azuki bean and the soya bean, plus the spectacular lab lab bean, with its purple and yellow flowers, and the yard-long bean which no gardener can resist growing, but which craves warmth to flourish and is best grown in the greenhouse or polytunnel.

Cucurbits

There are some very unfamiliar members of the cucumber family to be found here. From the smooth luffa to the hairy cucumber, the descriptions of them are fascinating to say the least.

Alliums

We are all familiar with Welsh onions; however, it appears that these have nothing to do with Wales but are in fact from the Orient! The mainstay of this group is the perennial bunching type of onions. The leafy shoots are used as chives, the bunching onions are used as spring onions and the taller growing varieties are earthed up and blanched like leeks. There is a type of Asiatic onion called *Rakkyo* that is grown in the same way as shallots but they may need two or three seasons to form sizable bulbs. The one member of the family that we already grow in large numbers is the hardy Japanese overwintering onion.

Roots and tubers

Included here are the radish and turnip, both of which are brassicas. The mooli radish that is grown for the winter is similar to the elongated white radish already grown in western gardens, but it can easily reach 60 cm (2 ft) in length! There are other radishes that resemble turnips and some that are grown for their tender leaves. There is even a radish that labours under the name of Rat's Tail. It is grown for its long tapering seed pods that resemble a rat's tail.

Japanese turnips can be small and round or long and slender, and they are eaten raw like a radish as well as being cooked.

More unusual is the Chinese yam which is a vigorous climbing plant that is grown for its edible club-shaped root that can be up to 1 metre (3 ft) in length. Most yams are too tender to grow in cooler temperate climates, but fortunately the Chinese yam is hardy. Also included in this group is the Chinese artichoke, which has been grown in western gardens for centuries.

There are many other exciting Oriental plants to grow, including chrysanthemum greens, amaranthus, Japanese burdock, Chinese celery and stem lettuce. All of them are easily raised from seed and will grow in the cooler regions.

Sprouting shoots
This term describes the pre-germinating of a variety of seeds from the above list of Oriental vegetable groups. They should be eaten almost as soon as they emerge or not long afterwards. To sprout the seeds, spread them over damp kitchen paper and place them somewhere warm until they germinate. Seed-sprouting containers can be bought for this purpose, or you can adapt plastic food containers or jam jars.

As the world grows smaller and cuisine becomes more cosmopolitan, we are now able to select and enjoy tastes from all around the world, and more importantly we can also grow, harvest and cook them ourselves. Oriental vegetables allow us to reach back thousands of years into history to a time when man began to tame and use to his advantage the food with which nature had surrounded him – it was the dawn of vegetable gardening.

Top tip

Oriental vegetables prefer cooler growing conditions, around 13–20°C (52–68°F). Don't be tempted to sow the seed of them until after the middle of the year.

Perennial vegetables

These are vegetable plants that are treated as herbaceous perennials. They can occupy a piece of ground for a very long time, as in the case of asparagus, or for no more than three years, in the case of globe artichokes.

Asparagus – *Asparagus officinalis*
Asparagus appreciates a well-drained soil. It is a maritime plant used to growing on sandy soils. Because it can occupy a site for up to 30 years, thorough soil preparation and weed eradication is essential before any planting takes place. Plants are usually bought in as one- or two-year-old crowns to speed up the planting to harvesting time.

Plant in March to April at a depth of 15 cm (6 inches). For April planting use one- or two-year-old crowns. Plant 45 cm (18 inches) apart with a distance of 60 cm (2 ft) between rows.

Harvest from late April or May until June, cutting the spears for no longer than six weeks. This is to give the crowns enough time to recover for the next year. Give the plants a top dressing of a general fertilizer to build up their strength. At the end of October cut down all of the top growth and put it on the compost heap. Cover the entire asparagus bed with well-rotted manure or compost.

Asparagus plants can also be raised from seed, but it will be at least three years before you will be able to cut any spears. One of the disadvantages of using seed-raised plants is that a number of them will be females producing seedlings that self-seed and grow between the rows of crowns, making them crowded and unproductive. Seed companies now offer male-only F1 Hybrid seed for sale to overcome this problem.

Sow under glass from February to March in the greenhouse. The seed can be sown in pots or trays filled with seed compost if you can maintain a temperature of 25°C (75°F). Prick the seedlings out into 9-cm (3.5-inch) pots filled with potting compost to grow on until they are large enough to plant out in nursery rows during April.

Sow outdoors in April in the open ground on a prepared seedbed. The seed is large enough to be sown at 15 cm (6 inch) apart in the row. Allow the plants to grow on for one season, planting them out in their final positions the following spring.

Chinese artichoke – *Stachys affinis*
The Chinese artichoke is an uncommon vegetable that grows under the soil, producing a small edible root tuber. The tuber has a buff skin with white flesh. It is only about 75 mm (3 inches) long and has a knobbly spiralled shape just like an extended sea shell. The roots are very brittle and break easily. Chinese artichokes have to be cleaned as soon as possible after lifting because if the soil dries on the root it is very difficult to remove.

Plant during the springtime at a depth of 10 cm (4 inches), 25 cm (10 inches) apart. Place three or four tubers together in a circle at each planting station. Leave a distance of 45 cm (18 inches) between rows.

Harvest from November to January, lifting them throughout the winter just before they are required. Chinese artichokes do not store well and go soft quite quickly.

Aftercare: Chinese artichokes are fairly undemanding. Keep them weed free and water regularly. Always keep some tuber for replanting.

Globe artichoke – *Cynara scolymus*

The globe artichoke is a vegetable that would not look out of place in the flower border. It is grown for its edible flower buds, but it also produces striking silver foliage that can be blanched before eating as a bonus. Globe artichokes can be raised from seed but the most reliable method of propagation is to buy in plants that are known to be sound croppers and increase your stock from these.

Sow seed from March to April in seed trays. It is always best to use a fresh site to grow globe artichokes every three years. They fit neatly to into any three-year rotation that includes strawberries.

Transplant offsets in October and March. The offsets or suckers are produced around the outside of the parent plant. To obtain offsets for transplanting, cut them away with a section of root still attached to the foliage. Plant them immediately and water regularly until established. Plant them 1 metre (3 ft) apart with the same distance between rows.

Harvest from July until October. Always cut heads before the scales start to turn purple and open. If you allow them to develop beyond this stage the flowering parts will begin to grow inside the head, making it unusable.

Aftercare: Top-dress all of the plants using a general fertilizer in the spring, and water often during dry spells to encourage plenty of growth. Clear away all decayed stems and foliage at the end of the season. In colder areas it may be safer to cover the crowns of the plants with straw or similar material.

Jerusalem artichoke – *Helianthus tuberosus*

Neither from Jerusalem nor an artichoke, but a sunflower that originates from North America, this is grown for its edible tuberous roots that resemble knobbly potatoes. They require careful siting in the garden because they make such tall plants, exceeding 2 metres (6 ft) in height. They will grow well in any reasonably fertile soil.

Plant from February to March at a depth of 15 cm (6 inches), 45 cm (18 inches) apart, with a distance of 1 metre (3 ft) between rows.

Harvest the tubers as required, digging them up and using them during October and November. They can also be lifted and stored in the same way as potatoes for use later in the winter.

Rhubarb – *Rheum rhaponticum*
When is a vegetable a fruit? When it is rhubarb! Grown for its red edible leaf stalks, it is always welcome as the first of the 'fruits' to come from a garden. It is a demanding plant because it requires moisture at the roots and its head in the sun.

Rhubarb can be grown from seed, but it is best to buy in named cultivars that are disease free.

Plant in March at a depth of 5 cm (2 inches) – just below the surface of the soil. Do not pick from them in their first year. Allow the crown to establish and build up for future seasons. Plant 1 metre (3 ft) apart, with the same distance between rows.

Harvest from March until late July, then stop cutting to allow the plants to recover. When harvesting the stalks, hold them with both hands, placing one near the bottom of the stalk and gently pulling, causing the entire stalk and leaf to snap away without damaging any developing shoots. The leaves are poisonous and should not be eaten in any form, but it is safe to compost them. Give the plants a top dressing of general fertilizer to help them recover.

Sea kale – *Crambe maritima*
Sea kale is a perennial member of the cabbage family and, as its name suggests, it likes to live by the sea. It has to be grown in a well-prepared soil containing plenty of organic matter.

Sea kale can be raised from seed but it is better to buy in root sections called 'thongs' to begin with. After this you can increase your stock by cutting away root sections to use as propagating material.

Plant in March or April at a depth of 12 mm (0.5 inches), just below the surface of the soil. Plant 1 metre (3 ft) apart, with the same distance between rows.

Harvest from February until March outdoors, or November until January indoors.

Aftercare: Sea kale has to be blanched before it can be used. To force it indoors, remove root sections during November, plunge them into pots filled with old potting compost or garden soil and place them somewhere dark. This could be under the greenhouse staging, or in a frost-free shed or outbuilding. Place five to seven root sections vertically in a 30-cm (12-inch) pot, with their tops set 5 cm (2 inches) above the surface of the compost. Place a pot of the same size over the roots and cover the drainage hole to shut out the light. In about five to six weeks the blanched stem should be 15 cm (6 inches) long and ready to cut.

Horseradish – *Armoracia rusticana*

Horseradish will grow almost anywhere provided that the soil is well drained. It has a very deep root system and needs a site that has been well cultivated to a depth of at least 60 cm (2 ft). It prefers to grow in full sun but will tolerate partial shade.

Horseradish is a rampant thug. If not managed ruthlessly it will completely overrun a garden. For this reason it may be best to grow it in a deep container to restrict the roots.

Caution

There have been reports of horses dying after eating too much horseradish foliage.

Plant in March using prepared root cutting/thongs, at a depth of 30 cm (12 inches). Make the planting holes with a crow bar. This will help to produce good straight roots for lifting. Drop the cuttings into the holes, setting the top of the cutting 5 cm (2 inches) below the surface of the soil, with a minimum distance of 60 cm (2 ft) each way between plants. Backfill around the cuttings with loose soil.

Harvest in autumn and winter. Wait until the plant has been frosted to improve the strength and flavour. Spring-planted roots could be large enough to cut at the end of their first season, but it is really better to wait until the end of their second year. To harvest the horseradish you can dig up the plant, cut off the roots and store them in boxes or containers of damp sand (or old potting soil), or leave the plant in the ground, cutting the roots as they are needed.

Propagation: Root cuttings known as thongs, 20 cm (8 inches) long by 2.5 cm (1 inch) in diameter, can be taken in the spring or autumn. The autumn cuttings are usually stored in damp sand or similar until required for planting during the following March. Thongs are prepared from sections of healthy young roots that are growing around the outside of the plant. To collect the cutting material the entire plant has to be dug up to reveal the root system.

Top tip

Once the root section has been cut away it will be difficult to remember which is the top and which the bottom. To avoid any confusion, make a horizontal cut at the top of the cutting and a sloping cut at the bottom.

A less common method of propagation is using crown cuttings. In the spring, just as growth is beginning to start, carefully lift up a section of the plant and cut away a section of root that has a young growth bud at the top. Trim the bottom of the crown root cutting and plant it out in a prepared bed. Water regularly until the plant is established. Replant the main root and water to settle back in.

Aftercare: All of the foliage will die down to soil level in the autumn when it can be cleared away and put on the compost heap.

Warning!

Do not throw any part of the root system on the compost heap. If you do it will be distributed all around the garden.

Greenhouse crops

Aubergines – *Solanum melongena*

This is known as the 'egg plant' because one member of the family produces white fruits that look like a hen's egg. The aubergine is very colourful. It also comes in purple, pink and black.

Sow from February to March under glass in gentle heat. Prick out the seedlings when they are large enough to handle into 9-cm (3.5-inch) flowerpots. Grow on until large enough pot up into a growing bag or a 15-cm (6-inch) pot containing general potting compost. They can be grown on in an unheated greenhouse in the same way as tomatoes.

Transplant only once all fear of frost has passed, and then only plant outside in the warmest part of the garden. Aubergines require a great deal of heat to grow outside. Plant 60 cm (2 ft) apart, with the same distance between rows.

Harvest from midsummer onwards.

Aftercare: Water and feed weekly with a high potash fertilizer. Misting over the plants with plain water will help the flowers set. Pinch out the growing tip of the plants when they are about 15 cm (6 inches) high. This will encourage four branches to develop and each branch will carry one fruit. Pick the fruit when it has developed the right colour.

Cucumbers – *Cucurbita sativus*

Cucumbers require high temperatures and very high humidity to grow successfully. They require a night temperature of at least 16°C (60°F). Another problem associated with the growing of cucumbers is bitterness of the fruits as a result of pollination of the flowers. The advice given is to remove all of the male flowers before the pollen can be transferred. It is easy to identify the male flower because it has no swollen seed capsule just behind the flower. To overcome this difficulty the gardener can now purchase all-female seed, completely removing the fear of producing bitter cucumbers.

Sow from February to March for growing in the heated greenhouse or April to grow in the unheated greenhouse. Sow one seed in 9-cm (3.5-inch) pots filled with seed compost. When sowing the seed, push it pointed-end downwards into the compost to a depth of 12 mm (0.5 inches), gently tapping the pot on the bench afterwards to cover over the seed. Water the pot and place it in a propagator set at 25°C (75°F).

Transplant when the roots of the cucumber plant have filled the pot. Transplant it into a growing bag or a 23-cm (9-inch) pot filled with potting compost. Do not plant too deeply to avoid neck rot of the stem. Plant 60 cm (2 ft), with a distance of 1 metre (3 ft) between rows.

Greenhouse cucumbers are grown using the single-stem or cordon method. Allow the main shoot to grow on, pinching out the growing tip when it reaches the ridge bar of the greenhouse. This will encourage side branches, known as laterals, to grow. It is on the laterals that the cucumbers will eventually develop. As the lateral grows it produces flowers that will become cucumbers. Pinch out the growing tip of the lateral two leaves beyond the flower. Remove any flowers or cucumbers that appear on the main stem.

Harvest from midsummer onwards.

Aftercare: Water and feed weekly with a high potash fertilizer. Spray the plants with plain water several times a day during the heat of summer. Apply shading to the greenhouse during May because cucumber plants have very sensitive leaves that will need protecting from the damaging rays of the midday sun. Spray water all over the plants and greenhouse in the morning and afternoon to create a humid atmosphere.

Peppers: sweet pepper – *Capsicum annuum* and chilli pepper – *Capsicum frutescens*

Peppers are best grown in the unheated greenhouse in cooler regions of the country. They require consistent temperatures to maintain steady growth. There are two types in general cultivation: the sweet, and the hot or chilli pepper. It is possible to grow the sweet peppers outdoors in warmer parts of the country but the chilli peppers require high humidity and are best grown in the greenhouse.

Sow from late February to March in heat for growing in the greenhouse. Sow late March for growing outdoors in favourable areas.

Prick out the seedlings when they are large enough to handle into 9-cm (3.5-inch) flower-pots. When they are large enough, pot on into 23-cm (9-inch) pots containing potting compost, or into small growing bags.

Transplant in June after the plants have been hardened off. Plant 60 cm (2 ft), with the same distance between rows. Some protection may be needed during the early stages of planting out.

Harvest from August onwards.

Aftercare: Water and feed weekly with a high potash liquid fertilizer. Pick off the first flowers to develop bushy plants.

Top tip

Pick off the first flowers on young pepper plants to encourage the development of side shoots: this will increase the number of peppers produced.

Top tip

The hot types of peppers can cause irritation or burning of the skin. Always take care to wash your hands after handling the fruits, especially the seeds.

Tomatoes – *Lycopersicon esclentum*

Tomatoes fall into two categories: *indeterminate* or cordon and *determinate* or bush. The cordon cultivars are grown in greenhouses and they can be grown outdoors as well. The bush types are always grown outdoors. Their sprawling habit makes them totally unsuitable for greenhouse cultivation.

Greenhouse tomatoes are ideal candidates for growing bags or 30-cm (12-inch) pots filled with potting compost. They can be grown in the soil of a greenhouse border but the soil will have to be exchanged for fresh garden soil every year to prevent the build up of soil-borne tomato pests and diseases.

Sow from February to March in gentle heat to grow in a cold greenhouse. Sow the seed in pots or trays filled with seed compost and cover lightly. Place in a propagator at a temperature of 18°C (65°F).

Prick out into 10-cm (4-inch) pots as soon as the seedlings produce their first rough leaves. Plant the seedling with the large seed leaves placed just above the surface of the compost. Water in to settle the plants and shade from direct sunlight for a few days. The young seedlings should be grown on a slightly lower temperature, around 16°C (60°F), to produce sturdy plants.

Transplant just as the young tomato plants begin to display their first truss of flowers. If they are planted before this stage they will continue to produce only leaves at the expense of flowers. It is important to get the first truss of flowers set (fertilized) to encourage the developing tomato plant to continue growing and produce further trusses. Plant 60 cm (2 ft) apart with a distance of 1 metre (3 ft) between rows.

Greenhouse tomatoes are grown as single stem cordons. To support them they can be tied to a bamboo cane or twisted around strong string that is suspended from the roof of the greenhouse.

When the young tomato plants are growing they will produce side shoots in the leaf axils. These must be removed as soon as these shoots are large enough to handle. If this is not done the plant will grow as a bush and not a single stem cordon. Pinch out the growing tip of the tomato plant when it has produced four or five trusses.

Harvest from late July onwards. The peak of the season is from late August until the end of September.

Aftercare: Water the plants regularly and do not start feeding them until the first truss has set. When you do feed them, use a high potash liquid fertilizer. Feed them weekly and gently tap the flower trusses around midday to help encourage the pollination of the flowers. Ventilate the greenhouse around mid-morning to prevent the inside temperatures getting too high and the atmosphere becoming too dry. Spray water all over the paths and floor of the greenhouse, using a watering can fitted with a fine rose, to lower the temperature and put moisture into the atmosphere.

Top tip

Place on overripe banana underneath tomato plants if the fruits are slow to turn from green to red.

Monthly list of produce available

	From the garden	Out of store
January	cabbage, sprouts, kale, leeks, carrots, parsnips, scorzonera, corn salad, winter spinach, salsify, Witloof chicory (forced), endive, radish, winter cauliflower	potatoes, beetroot, celeriac, celery, carrots, onions, blanched chicory, garlic, shallots, Jerusalem artichoke, turnips, swedes, cabbage
February	cabbage, sprouts, kale, leeks, carrots, parsnips, scorzonera, broccoli, winter spinach, salsify, endive, radish, sea kale, Witloof chicory (forced), corn salad, winter cauliflower	potatoes, beetroot, carrots, onions, garlic, shallots, turnips, swedes, celeriac, Jerusalem artichoke, celery

	From the garden	Out of store
March	leeks, sprouting broccoli, spring cabbage, kale, parsnips, sea kale, blanched chicory, chard, lettuce (leaves), winter cauliflower, spring onions (winter)	potatoes, carrots, onions, beetroot, Jerusalem artichoke, parsnips, turnips, swedes
April	asparagus, sprouting broccoli, spring cabbage, early carrots, cauliflower, lettuce, radish, beetroot, spring onions, turnips, broad beans, chard, chives	leeks, onions, swedes, turnips
May	asparagus, sprouting broccoli, carrots, early peas, lettuce, beetroot, turnips, cabbage, radish, spring onions, spinach, broad beans, chives	
June	asparagus, cabbage, beetroot, lettuce, radish, spring onions, peas, chard, spinach, carrots, new potatoes, cauliflower, turnips, broad beans, bunching onions, marrow, cucumber, chives, Japanese onions, endive	
July	aubergine, tomatoes, lettuce, beetroot, peas, broad beans, French beans, carrots, spinach, spinach beet, shallots, garlic, onions, bunching onions, turnips, kohlrabi, new potatoes, chard, globe artichoke, marrow, courgette, cucumber, pumpkins, chives, sweet corn, endive, calabrese	

August	aubergine, tomatoes, peppers, courgette, carrots, calabrese, shallots, bunching onions, garlic, onions, lettuce, spinach, spinach beet, peas, French beans, runner beans, peas, beetroot, turnips, chard, potatoes, kohlrabi, globe artichoke, marrow, Chinese greens, cucumber, pumpkins, chives, sweetcorn, endive, Hamburg parsley	garlic, shallots
September	aubergine, pepper, tomato, runner beans, French beans, carrots, calabrese, beetroot, chard, bunching onions, endive, potatoes, kohlrabi, sugar loaf chicory, chicory, lettuce, globe artichoke, cauliflower, marrow, courgette, spinach, spinach beet, Chinese greens, turnips, cucumber, pumpkins, chives, sweetcorn, Hamburg parsley	garlic, shallots, onions
October	tomato, pepper, runner beans, French beans, globe artichoke, carrots, cabbage, turnips, celery, celeriac, potatoes, beetroot, bunching onions, endive, radish, kohlrabi, sugar loaf chicory, chicory, lettuce, swede, broccoli, cauliflower, Chinese	garlic, shallots, onions

	greens, marrow, spinach beet, corn salad, pumpkins, chives, calabrese, Hamburg parsley	
November	cabbage, Brussels sprouts, broccoli, leeks, parsnips, carrots, celery, celeriac, swede, radish, Jerusalem artichoke, spinach beet, celery, corn salad, endive, kale	potatoes, beetroot, onions, marrow, pumpkin, garlic, shallots, tomatoes, celeriac, turnips, swedes, haricot beans
December	Brussels sprouts, cabbage, kale, leeks, parsnips, carrots, salsify, scorzonera, spinach beet, celery, corn salad, endive	Jerusalem artichoke, potatoes, beetroot, onions, garlic, shallots, celeriac, marrow, pumpkin, turnips, swedes, cabbage, haricot beans

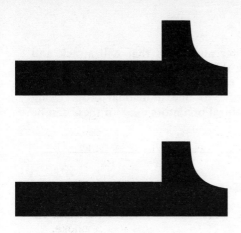

common pests and diseases

In this chapter you will learn:
- which pests attack specific crops
- which diseases can affect crops
- how to prevent and control pests and diseases.

Pests

There are pests such as slugs and snails that will attack and destroy almost any crop in the garden. Some, such as aphids, will attack a wide variety of crops while others, such as the asparagus beetle, are specific to one individual crop. Using careful management and natural predators most of these can be kept under control.

Top tip

Don't release biological predators until the pest to be controlled is present.

Diseases

Many diseases that affect plants are either fungal or viral. Fungal spores, such as potato blight, are airborne, so avoid overcrowding crops and allow a good flow of air between plants. There are also soil-borne diseases such as brassica club root. Viruses are mainly transmitted from plant to plant by aphids and other types of sap-sucking insects. They can also be carried via contaminated knives and secateurs.

This chapter contains descriptions of some of the more common pests and diseases that are likely to be encountered in the vegetable garden.

Potatoes

Potato blackleg

The foliage of the potato is stunted and becomes pale yellow. This is sometimes confused with potato blight but is easily identified by the blackening of the base of the potato haulm (foliage), which eventually causes it to rot away. It can be caused by damaging the plants and allowing bacteria to enter the wound. It is always worse in a wet summer. Grow blackleg resistant cultivars.

Wireworm

This is a small yellowish grub about 25 mm (1 inch) long that has three pairs of legs at its head end. It lives in the soil and bores small holes into the potato tuber. It is usually only a problem on freshly cultivated grassland or soil that has been left neglected for a long time. You can trap them by pushing sections of carrot into the soil to attract the wireworms. You can then collect these and dispose of them, destroying the pest at the same time. Regular cultivation of the soil will quickly eliminate wireworms.

Potato cyst eelworm

This is a very serious potato pest. Eelworms are small nematodes (worms) that attack and feed on the root system of potatoes. The earliest sign of a problem is when the foliage begins to turn yellow from the bottom upwards. In a heavy infestation the potato produces very small tubers and the plants may die. Always use certified seed potatoes and wash them in warm water before setting them up for chitting (see Chapter 10, page 101). The female lives within the potato root system before bursting through the root wall to lay her eggs in the soil. The young nematodes hatch and feed on the roots. The eggs can remain active in the soil for up to ten years. It will be impossible to grow potatoes on any ground that has a serious infestation of eelworm.

Modern potato breeding programmes are developing eelworm-resistant varieties.

Slugs

Slugs are always a problem where soil conditions are wet and heavy. Grow early varieties and make sure you lift them before September. This will usually give slug-free crops.

Top tip

Place a scooped-out half of an orange or grapefruit on the soil where you expect plants to suffer from slugs and snails. They will crawl inside and remain there. Check daily and destroy any slugs or snails that are found.

Scab

This is only a problem on alkaline soil. Digging in organic matter will go some way towards controlling it. The unpleasant appearance is only skin deep – it does not have any effect on the quality of the crop. Scab-resistant varieties are now beginning to appear in catalogues more frequently.

Blight

This is probably the biggest problem with potatoes. It is always more severe during warm wet summers when humidity is high. The fungal spores are transported by rain, which makes the foliage extremely vulnerable to attack. In recent seasons potato blight has been seen earlier and earlier, sometimes arriving during July. As soon as the telltale brown spots can be seen on the leaves, completely remove and destroy all of the foliage. It is important to prevent the spores from contaminating the soil where they can quickly infest the developing potato tubers.

Dark sunken patches develop on the skin of the potato tuber and when the tuber is cut open you will see a discolouration of the flesh. This will eventually cause the tuber to rot, giving off a very unpleasant smell. Do not be tempted to store blighted tubers and never save them for using as seed potatoes. Always buy fresh certified stock each season to reduce the risk of introducing potato blight to the soil. A combination of using crop rotation and growing the more blight-resistant cultivars that are now available should help to control the problem.

Carrots

Carrot root fly

These are 12-mm (0.5-inch) long maggots that tunnel into the carrot roots, making them unusable. Most of the damage occurs during late summer. This pest can completely destroy a crop. The fly is at its most active during May and June, so you can avoid too much damage by varying sowing dates. Make the earliest sowings during March to provide a crop in June to August. Follow on by sowing the main crop during late June/July. In both cases sow the seed as thinly as possible to avoid having to over-thin afterwards. The scent of the freshly crushed foliage attracts the female fly, inviting her to lay her eggs in the soil near the crop. Thinning after rain or in the cool of the evening helps to fool her. Also try watering along the rows before thinning. One tip that works is to keep drawing soil up over the shoulders of the carrots, always leaving a tuft of foliage to grow on.

> **Top tip**
>
> Try growing a row or two of scorzonera with carrots to deter attack from carrot root fly. If you have recurring problems with carrot root fly try growing the yellow cultivars as they seem to suffer less.

Wireworm

These can be a problem on recently broken ground. You can achieve some control by growing early, fast-maturing varieties and harvesting them when young. After the first season the wireworms should not be a problem.

Splitting

This is the result of erratic watering. Soak the row well at least once a week during dry conditions. When carrots are grown in good soil that contains plenty of organic material splitting of the carrot roots it is not too much of a problem.

Always select a variety to suit the soil conditions: short stump-rooted types for hard, stony ground; long tapering roots can only be produced in fibrous soils.

Other root vegetables

Beetroot

These are a fairly trouble-free crop. Avoid damaging the swollen roots when hoeing along the rows and water regularly to prevent them becoming 'woody' and unusable.

They can be susceptible to scab, when the roots will appear to have a sunken scabby patches and/or scabby raised areas. Although these look unpleasant the roots are perfectly usable. This disease is usually worse in light soils.

Parsnips

The main pest of parsnips is the celery leaf miner. It tunnels between the layers of leaf tissue, leaving a telltale raised track in the leaf. Any time after May, brown blisters appear on the leaves. Remove the infested leaves, crushing them before they are destroyed, then give the plants a liquid feed to boost re-growth.

Turnips

The only real problem for this crop is flea beetle during hot, dry spells. It is easily controlled by watering along the rows of seedling during the cool of the evening. Sometimes known as turnip fly, flea beetle will attack the seed leaves of all brassicas. It is not a problem once the rough true leaves are produced.

Onions

Onion fly

This is without doubt the most serious pest for all members of the onion family. Most of the damage is done around May to June time when the female fly is active and laying her eggs at the base of the plant. After hatching, the 9-mm long maggots feed on the onion bulb roots, causing the plant to collapse. Dig up the entire plant and destroy it by burning; also inspect the root area to ensure that no larvae have survived in the soil.

Onion mildew

This appears as grey/purplish streaks or spots on the foliage of the plants. It is more disfiguring than damaging. It is usually worse during mild, wet seasons. Planting at 30-cm (12-inch) spacings will help to improve the air circulation around the growing plants and thus lessen the chances of an attack.

Onion neck rot

This is a fungus disease that will destroy onions that are being kept in store. Always ensure that all onion bulbs are properly dried and ripened before storing away. It can be caused by bending the tops over before the bulb is fully grown. Always wait for the foliage to collapse in its own time before lifting the onion bulbs. Growing from heat-treated sets and always using fresh seed will help to prevent an attack.

Onion white rot

This is probably the most serious disease of onions. A white fluffy mould develops on the roots and base of the onion bulb. The foliage turns yellow and then shrivels. It will be impossible to grow any member of the onion family on the infected ground. White rot is a fungal disease that can live in the soil for up to 15 years. There is no chemical cure or control available to the amateur gardener. The only solution is to grow onions on a clean fresh site.

Leeks, shallots and garlic

Generally leeks are free from serious pests and diseases. They may suffer from mildew (see onions, above). Onion pests and diseases also apply to shallots and garlic.

Leeks may suffer from rust, when bright orange elongated pustules of spores can be seen on the leaves. There is no control available, so always take great care to remove and burn all infected leaves. Rotate the site each season. Although the plants can look unsightly the leeks are perfectly edible. It is more of a problem for the exhibitor.

Other vegetables

Globe artichokes

Petal blight fungus will cause the artichoke heads to rot. Avoid over-feeding the plants, which will produce soft vulnerable tissue. Remove all spent foliage at the end of the season.

Broad beans

Black bean aphid (blackfly)
The black bean aphid will attack all members of the bean family. The aphid itself is about 3 mm ($^1/_8$ of an inch) long. They are a real problem because they will form sticky clusters of blackfly all over the stems, leaves and tips of the plants. If natural predators are unable to cope with a heavy infestation, spray with an insecticidal soap (Savona) until the natural balance has returned. Sometimes pinching out the tips of plants as they come into flower will check the pest, allowing the pods to swell. Making early sowings during February will produce plants with tips that become tough and unattractive to aphids.

> **Top tip**
> Sprinkle fine dry soil over young bean plants to control attacks of blackfly.

Bean chocolate spot

This is a fungus disorder that causes dark chocolate brown spots to develop on the leaves, stems and pods of the broad bean plants. The fungus spores can be carried on the seeds or may overwinter in the garden on the remains of old plants. It is always made worse by damp humid conditions. Always ensure that the site is well drained and free from the shade of overhanging trees or buildings. Encourage a good air circulation around the plants by planting the beans at 30-cm (12-inch) spacings with at least 45 cm (18 inches) between double rows.

Runner beans and dwarf French beans

As with broad beans, these will suffer with black bean aphid (blackfly). If natural predators are unable to cope with outbreaks then spray with insecticidal soap (Savona) until balance is restored.

Runner beans and dwarf French beans may also suffer from root rot. You can control this by rotating crops and growing on a fresh site each season.

Top tip

Do not cultivate around beans after rainfall or early in the day when the foliage is wet. The dampness helps to transmit bean rust and other diseases such as bean mosaic.

Peas

Foot rot

This will damage plants. To prevent this, avoid creating heavy wet soil conditions. Early varieties are especially vulnerable. A simple control is to change the site each season.

Powdery mildew

This is a fungal problem of later maturing varieties that causes the leaves to turn yellow and then develop a grey fungal growth. It can be caused by dryness at the roots, so prepare moisture-retentive soil that is not waterlogged. Also remove the spent haulms of earlier sown varieties: these can act as host plants for mildew. Try growing mildew-resistant cultivars of peas.

Pea moth

The small white pea moth caterpillar eats the peas while they are
still in the pod. You can control it by growing pea varieties that
do not flower during June and mid-August when the moth is
most active. An alternative for continued production is to grow
mangetout varieties.

Aphid (greenfly)

If natural predators such as ladybirds and hoverflies are unable
to cope with the aphid infestation, spray with insecticidal soap
until the natural balance is restored.

Thrips

These are small black 3-mm ($^1/_8$ of an inch) beetles that are
active during the early summer. The foliage becomes discoloured
and the pods display silvery marks along them. When peas are
attacked by thrips the developing pods will only produce a few
small peas at the stalk end of the pod. These sap-sucking insects
are more of a problem in hot dry summers.

Pea and bean weevil

The only damage is a slight scalloping of the leaf edges. It is
caused by a greyish brown beetle that lives in the soil and feeds
on the nitrogenous root nodules The weevils are only ever
active at soil level, and once the plants begin to grow away the
problem is over.

Top tip

To stop mice stealing recently sown pea seed try soaking the
seeds in a mixture of seaweed fertilizer a couple of hours before
sowing them.

Brassicas

Flea beetle

These are small black beetles that always jump when they are
disturbed. They are mainly active during spring and late
summer. They will attack the seed leaves of *all* members of the
brassica family, leaving small holes in them. Flea beetles are only
a problem in dry weather and you can control them by watering
the foliage during the cool of the evening. Once the true leaves
begin to grow the problem will cease.

Cabbage root fly

These small white maggots 9 mm (0.4 inches) long attack the root systems of *all* members of the brassica family. They are mainly active during spring and early summer. They usually attack cabbages and cauliflowers soon after planting out. The first sign of an attack is the plant collapsing, and when it is dug up it has no roots. The eggs are laid just below the surface of the soil quite close to the plant. They hatch out and the maggots feed on the roots and tunnel into the stems to pupate.

Placing a 15-cm (6-inch) collar at soil level is usually sufficient protection to prevent an attack. The collar can be made from a flexible material such as carpet underlay or felt material. Cut a 15-cm (6-inch) disc out of the material and then make a cut that reaches the centre of the collar. This will allow for a snug fit around the stem of the plant and remove any risk of eggs being laid close to the plant. Make sure that the disc is always in close contact with the surface of the soil to be effective; places stones around the edge to keep it in place. The eggs will be laid at the edge of the collar and the maggots will perish before they can begin to feed on the roots and stem of the plant.

If any plants are attacked, dig the entire plant out and destroy it by burning. Check the soil to make sure no maggots remain there.

figure 11.1 a brassica collar

Cabbage whitefly

These are very small white flying insects that hide away on the undersides of brassica leaves. They suck the sap of the plants and produce an unpleasant black sticky deposit that is called honeydew or 'sooty mould'. This can affect the ability of the leaf to function properly. Cabbage whiteflies are difficult to control but fortunately the damage is mainly to the outside leaves, which you can remove and destroy to kill the pest. Spraying regularly with insecticidal soap will help to keep them under control. Remove all overwintering brassica plants from the garden as soon as possible in the late winter/early spring to prevent them infesting newly planted out brassicas.

Cabbage aphid
Spray these with insecticidal soap as soon as they are seen. Once they get under the heart leaves they are impossible to control.

Cabbage white butterflies
There are two types of large cabbage butterfly: one is white, the other is yellow with black markings. Both the large and small cabbage white butterfly lay their yellow eggs in small clusters on the undersides of the brassica leaves. The caterpillars of the large butterflies have yellow and black bands; the small butterfly and cabbage moth caterpillars are green.

The caterpillars of the large butterflies feed mainly on the outer leaves and the caterpillars of the small white butterflies and moth eat their way into the hearts of brassicas. It is the late summer broods that cause all the problems. To deal with small infestations, crush the eggs by hand and pick off the caterpillars. Use *bacillus thuruginensis* (BT) to control larger colonies. It comes in powder form and is mixed with water to spray on to the leaves.

Carry out a soil check to confirm what remedial action needs to be taken. Usually all that is required is a dressing of ground chalk or lime. Calcified seaweed also has a high pH.

Club root
This is sometimes called 'finger and toe' disease because the root system of the plant becomes stunted and swollen. It can affect all members of the brassica family. The first visible symptoms are the collapse of the plant during the day, with it appearing to recover during the cool of the night. When the plant is dug up the swollen root system can be seen. Club root is a type of slime mould that flourishes in poorly drained and acid soils. Carry out a soil check to confirm what remedial action needs to be taken. Usually all that is required is a dressing of ground chalk or lime. Calcified seaweed also has a high pH. Improving the drainage and liming the soil to raise the pH to above 6.5 will help to overcome the problem.

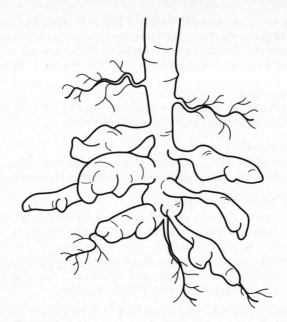

figure 11.2 club root

It is safest to raise your own brassica plants and never be tempted to accept well-intended gifts of plants from other gardeners.

Birds

Erect some form of net caging to cover the crop until it is harvested. There is a wide variety of bird scarers available. They will have to be used sparingly because the birds will quickly become accustomed to them.

Spinach

Mildew is the main problem of spinach. This is usually caused through dryness at the roots or overcrowding of the plants. Thin the plants to at least 30 cm (12 inches) apart and make sure that the rows are kept well watered.

Celery and celeriac

Leaf miner/fly

This is the main pest of celery and related plants such as parsnips. It tunnels between the layers of leaf tissue, leaving a telltale raised track in the leaf. Any time after May, brown blisters appear on the leaves. Remove the infested leaves, crushing them before they are destroyed, then give the plants a liquid feed to boost re-growth.

Leaf spot
This can be identified by the brown patches that appear on the leaves and stems of the plants. It usually is a seed-borne disease so always buy clean, reliable seed.

Lettuces

Aphid (greenfly)
Spray with an insecticidal soap to control heavy infestations of greenfly, or wash the heads thoroughly before eating.

Mildew
This is a grey fluffy mould that attacks the leaves and stem of lettuces. Sometimes the plants are attacked at soil level and rot off. Avoid planting too deeply and make sure that the soil is well prepared before planting out.

Tomatoes – under glass and outdoors

Blight
This is exactly the same blight as that which attacks potatoes, so avoid growing tomatoes on land that previously grew potatoes. Grow the more modern resistant cultivars to avoid having to use copper-based fungicides. In recent years a citrus-based product has offered some control.

Blossom end rot
A small dark sunken patch develops at the base of the developing tomato fruit. It is a physiological disorder and does not spread among the plants. This is a common problem of tomatoes grown under glass as well as outdoors. It is caused by irregular watering, especially when the fruit is first developing. Take care to water the tomato plants regularly after the first truss of fruits has set. There is no control other than watering. Remove any affected tomatoes to prevent the plant from wasting its energy.

Greenback
This is a hard dark-green patch that develops around the stalk of the fruit. It is caused by high levels of sunlight which damage

the tissue of the fruit. Providing shade for the plants will help to control it. Regular feeding with a high potash fertilizer will also give some protection.

Fruits splitting

The skin of the tomato fruit splits open spoiling its table qualities. This is caused by erratic growth and too-high temperatures around the plants.

Asparagus

Asparagus beetle is the main pest. The adult beetle is about 6 mm (0.25 inches) long and has a black body with yellow squared markings. The larvae are grey and yellow and can be mistaken for ladybird larvae at first.

The attacks start in May/June when the winged adult lays small black eggs on the asparagus foliage. Both the larvae and adult feed on the foliage. In extreme cases they will completely defoliate the plant. Spray with insecticidal soap to control. You can also hand pick and destroy them. At the end of October, cut off all of the ferny leaves and destroy them to kill off any surviving beetles.

Sweetcorn

The main problem for sweetcorn is frit fly larvae. They will burrow into the tips of growing plants, which stunts their growth and produces twisted or damaged leaves. Try spraying with insecticidal soap. Sow under glass during April to avoid attacks to seed sown in open ground during May.

Cucumbers marrows and courgettes

Cucumber mosaic virus

This commonly affects all members of the family, especially marrows. Affected plants have puckered, distorted leaves that are yellow with dark-green patches. Remove and destroy these plants before they infect other plants around them. The virus has many host plants, especially weeds, so it is essential to keep the plot as weed free as possible. Aphids act as vectors (transmitters of the disease), so spray with insecticidal soap to control them.

Powdery mildew

This is usually caused by dryness at the roots. Water the plants regularly to prevent them from becoming stressed.

Florence fennel

Generally Florence fennel is trouble free. It can be prone to bolting under cold or dry conditions. Sowing the seed too early in the summer can make the problem worse. Wait until late May or early June before making the earliest sowings.

Top tip

Place a glass jam jar or pot filled with dry grass, straw or newspaper to trap earwigs. Check daily and burn the contents to destroy any pests.

Top tip

Try baiting mousetraps with melon seeds. They just can't resist them.

12

herbs

The cultivation of herbs

The cultivation of herbs always conjures up images of apothecaries dispensing mysterious potions that were created to heal and cure. This is because herbs were originally grown in botanical gardens where the plants would be grown in groups according to their use. Out of these botanical gardens emerged the Physick Garden, where the plants were grown for the express purposes of research into their healing properties. However, for the purposes of this book we shall be concentrating only on culinary garden herbs that are in common cultivation today. Medicinal and healing herbs belong to a different branch of horticulture and should only be used with care.

Herbs are thought to be able to survive and grow almost anywhere, but this is not the case and, like all other plants, herbs have their own special growing needs if they are to flourish. Many of the varieties of herbs which we are familiar with today were first introduced by the Romans, and that should give a clue to their cultivation needs. Mediterranean countries are extremely hot and the soil is gritty and free draining, but there is always a plentiful supply of underground water available.

The most common advice given is to grow your herbs as near to the house as possible because this allows them to be picked and taken to the kitchen in the freshest possible condition. This is not always possible, however, and herbs are grown on vegetable plots, in flower borders or on allotments. As long as they are picked in the peak of condition they will always be full of favour and fit to use in the kitchen. The herb plot does not have to be large – it is surprising what an area as small as 2 × 3 metres (6 × 10 ft) will yield.

Something that you should consider before you begin any planting is that herbs can either be perennial, such as sage and rosemary, or annuals like dill, coriander and chervil, which will be harvested before the summer has ended. Growing the annual forms in the flower border will leave you with unwanted gaps. The perennials, of course, will occupy their site for many years – some of them can be up to 2 metres (6 ft) tall while others are 'spreaders', so you will need to allocate them with sufficient room in the garden to develop to their ultimate size.

Remember also that some herbs need a moisture-retentive soil and others require a gritty, free-draining loamy soil. If they are to succeed, both groups need to be grown on a sunny open site that is free from overhanging trees and shadows from tall buildings.

Descriptive list and cultivation notes

There follows a descriptive list and cultivation notes of the most commonly used herbs in the kitchen. The Latin names have been included to avoid any possible confusion with other members of the herb family.

Angelica – *Angelica archangelica*

Biennial/short-lived perennial.

Height and spread: 2.5 metres (8 ft).

Situation: Semi-shade; grow in a moisture-holding soil that is high in organic matter.

Harvesting: Cut young leaf stalks during mid-spring before they become tough and stringy.

Aftercare: Remove flower stalks/heads as they appear, to prolong the life of the plant.

Propagation: Seed may be collected, dried and sown as soon as possible after flowering.

Flavour: Hint of vanilla.

Use: The tender, young green stalks are crystallized to be used as a confection.

Basil – *Ocimum basilicum/Ocimum minimum*

Tender annual.

Height and spread: 60 cm (2 ft).

Situation: Warm and sheltered; best when grown in greenhouse border or flowerpot. Prefers a good loamy soil. Try to avoid root disturbance.

Harvesting: Cut fresh leaves as required throughout the summer.

Aftercare: Pinch out tips of shoots to create a bushy plant and remove flowers as they appear. At the end of summer pull and dispose of plant on the compost heap.

Propagation: Sow seed in pots in the greenhouse during the spring. Plant out when all fear of frost has gone.

Flavour: Mild aniseed.

Use: Basil goes well with tomatoes, cheese, eggs and pizzas; it is an essential ingredient of pesto sauce.

Bay – *Laurus nobilis*

Woody, evergreen perennial.

Height and spread: 2 m (6 ft). Can be restricted to 1.5 m (5 ft) in a pot or container, but it can grow into a small tree if planted in the open ground.

Site and soil: Plant during the spring. If growing in the open ground, select a sunny and open site, sheltered from strong winds and frost. Any reasonably fertile soil will be good enough. If a small and more manageable tree is required it is best to grow the tree in the smallest pot that is practical, allowing the roots to become almost pot bound before re-potting into a pot the next size up. Bay is always best when grown outdoors so place container-grown plants outside during the summer, bringing them indoors for the winter.

Harvesting: Pick leaves sparingly during the first few years while the plant is establishing itself; after that use as required.

Aftercare: Water the young plant regularly in the first years. During the late spring or early summer, pinch out the tips of young shoots to keep the plant in shape. Feed container-grown plants regularly during the growing season. Do not allow the plant to dry out at any time.

Pests and diseases: Scale insects.

Propagation: Heel cuttings that are taken in the autumn. Select a healthy young shoot about 1 m (3 ft) in length and tear it gently from the branch so that it comes away with a sliver of bark from the main branch. Trim the 'heel' and push the cutting into moist sandy compost. Place somewhere cool and shady to produce roots and pot on at a later date.

Flavour: Strong, pungent.

Use: Add to a bouquet garni or use separately in many stew-type dishes.

Caraway – *Carum carus*

Biennial.

Height and spread: 60 cm (2 ft).

Site and soil: Will tolerate partial shade but not a waterlogged soil. If the soil is heavy, dig in sharp grit to improve the drainage.

Harvesting: The flower heads that yield the seeds are produced in the second year. Cut the seed heads when the stems begin to discolour and while they are still green, then place them into a paper bag and hang them up to dry and split open. Store the seeds in a dry airtight container until required.

Aftercare: Water the young plants regularly to prevent them from running to seed in the first year. If they are wanted, the young leaves can be cut lightly in the first year; otherwise just concentrate on building the plant up for seed production in the second year.

Propagation: Seed, sown in the open ground during April/May. Sow thinly in rows 45 cm (18 inches) apart, thinning to 45 cm (18 inches) later. Because caraway produces a long tap root it is unsuitable for transplanting. If it is to be grown in a container, sow several seeds spaced out in a group and then thin down to one to grow on.

Flavour: Distinctive, very aromatic, strong flavouring.

Use: Baking, flavouring.

Chervil – *Anthriscus cerefolium*
Hardy annual – the curly leafed variety is the best.

Height and spread: 45 cm (18 inches).

Site and soil: Appreciates semi-shade and a moisture-holding soil. Too much sun causes it to run to seed which will reduce the flavour of the leaves.

Propagation: Seed, sown in the open ground during April/May and August. Leave 30 cm (12 inches) between the rows, thinning to 30 cm (12 inches) in the row. Keep the young plants well watered.

Aftercare: Keep well watered at all times.

Harvesting: Cut down and gather the leaves just as the plant reaches its full height; this will also delay flowering. To maintain a steady supply all summer long, make successional sowings monthly during April and May.

Flavour: Similar to parsley but with a peppery/aniseedy taste.

Use: As a garnish but it can also be used as a flavouring, particularly with fish dishes.

Coriander – *Coriandrum sativum*

Hardy annual.

Height and spread: 45 cm (18 inches).

Site and soil: Full sun, good free-draining loamy soil.

Propagation: Seed, sown under glass in early spring to transplant outside later, or directly into the soil in late spring when it has warmed up. It may also be sown in the early autumn to overwinter with protection. Sow in shallow drills 30 cm (12 inches) apart, thinning to 30 cm (12 inches) in the row.

Aftercare: Keep the plot weed free and water regularly.

Harvesting: The seeds ripen and fall very quickly, so be ready to harvest them as soon as they become a beige colour. Tie the heads together and hang them somewhere dark over sheets of paper to catch the seeds. The young leaves may be used as a parsley substitute.

Flavour: Hint of orange.

Use: Curries, chutney and fish dishes.

Dill – *Anthum graveolens*

Annual.

Height and spread: 90 cm (3 ft).

Site and soil: Full sun, good free-draining loam.

Propagation: Seed, sow directly into the open ground. Dill produces a tap root and resents any form of disturbance that will check its growth. Sow in shallow drills 30 cm (12 inches) apart and thin to 30 cm (12 inches) in the row. Water along the rows of thinned plants to settle them back into the soil.

Aftercare: Water regularly. The plants will require some form of support when they are almost fully grown.

Harvesting: The leaves must be cut as soon as possible, while the plants are still young. After two months or so the flower heads will be produced. Remove the flower heads if any more leaf growth is required; otherwise, allow the seeds to ripen until they turn dark brown and are then ready to harvest. Gather the seed heads and hang them somewhere dark and dry over sheets of newspaper to catch the seed.

Flavour: Aniseedy.

Use: Fish dishes and pickles.

Fennel – *Foeniculum vulgare*
Perennial.

Height and spread: 1.5 m (5 ft).

Site and soil: Full sun, good free-draining loam.

Propagation: Usually brought in as pot-grown plants. If extra plants are required, fennel can be divided and potted up in the autumn to be grown on under protection to be planted out the following spring. Plants can also be raised from seed sown in late April/May. Sow in shallow drills and thin to 60 cm (2 ft) apart in the rows to transplant the following spring.

Aftercare: Water regularly and keep the plot weed free. Place some support around the plant when it is almost fully grown.

Harvesting: Cut the young leaves until the flower heads are produced; remove the flower heads if more leaves are required. If fennel seeds are needed then allow the plant to flower and collect the seeds when they begin to turn brown. Hang the seed heads somewhere dry over paper to catch the seed.

Flavour: Liquorice.

Use: Both leaves and seed can be used with fish dishes.

Lovage – *Levisticum officinale*
Perennial.

Height and spread: 2 m (6 ft).

Site and soil: Lovage will tolerate a certain amount of shade. It requires a good, rich moisture-holding loam soil.

Propagation: Usually brought in as a pot-grown plant in the spring. Can be grown from fresh seed sown in small pots or trays in the autumn, then pricked out into 9-cm (3.5-inch) pots when large enough to handle singly. These are then grown on through the winter, protected in a frame or greenhouse to be planted out in the spring. Mature plants can be lifted and divided in the early autumn.

Aftercare: Lovage is virtually a bog plant, so it needs large amounts of water. Never allow it to become dry at the roots. It will need staking when fully grown.

Harvesting: Clip young leaves from the plant throughout the growing season. They can be used fresh or dried.

Use: The leaves and stems can be used to add a celery flavour to soups, casseroles and stews.

Marjoram/oregano
There are various varieties:

Origanum vulgare – wild marjoram; usually called 'Oregano'
Hardy perennial.

Height and spread: 75 cm (2.5 ft).

Origanum onites – pot marjoram
Hardy perennial.

Height and spread: 45 cm (18 inches).

Origanum majorana – sweet marjoram
Half-hardy annual.

Height and spread: 20 cm (8 inches).

For all varieties:

Site and soil: Full sun, free-draining soil.

Propagation: Seed, sown in open ground during April. Sow seed in shallow drills 30 cm (12 inches) apart. Grow on to transplant later in the summer. May also be propagated from divisions in the spring.

Aftercare: Water well until established. Pot marjoram can be lifted before leaf fall, cut back by half, potted up and taken indoors to maintain a winter supply. The sweet marjoram will not survive the winter. Pull it up and put it on the compost heap.

Harvesting: The leaves will be ready for harvesting towards the end of summer. They can be stored in an airtight container.

Flavour: Pine/citrus.

Use: The wild form is used on pizzas; pot and sweet marjoram are used in soups and with lamb.

Mint – *Mentha species*
Hardy perennial.

Height and spread: 45+ cm (18+ inches); mints are very invasive and there is no limit to their spread.

Site and soil: Semi-shade, good moisture-holding loam. All members of the mint family require a cool moist soil.

Propagation: Usually brought in as pot-grown plants. They are very easy to propagate from cuttings taken at any time or from root section cuttings.

Aftercare: Keep well watered. Mint spreads rapidly by sending out underground roots. To keep it under control, chop around the plant with a spade to cut off the unwanted roots. It is best grown in a large pot/container but will need replacing every two to three years.

Harvesting: Cut fresh leaves from the plant throughout the growing season. If needed for drying, collect the leaves before flowering time.

Use: Fresh mint is used with garden peas and new potatoes. Mint sauce is used on roast lamb.

Parsley – *Petroselinium crispum*
Biennial.

There are several varieties of parsley.

Height and spread: 30 cm (12 inches).

Site and soil: Full sun, good moisture-holding loam.

Propagation: Seed, sown under glass in March to grow on and be planted out after the fear of frost has gone. Seed may be sown in the open ground but it can be difficult to germinate. To maintain an all-year round supply, sow one batch in the spring and a second around midsummer.

Aftercare: Never allow parsley to go short of water as it will run to seed very quickly. Cloches should be placed over the plants to protect them during the winter.

Harvesting: Cut fresh young leaves as required throughout the growing season. Parley leaves can be dried and stored in airtight containers.

Flavour: Fresh/iron.

Use: Fresh leaves are used as garnishes and parsley sauce is used with fish dishes.

Rosemary – *Rosmarinus officinalis*
Hardy evergreen perennial.

Height and spread: 1.5 m (5 ft).

Site and soil: Full sun, free-draining gritty loam. Rosemary will not tolerate waterlogged conditions.

Propagation: Usually brought in as a pot-grown plant. Heel cuttings can be taken during May, June and July. Once rooted grow on in 9-cm (3-inch) pots until large enough to plant out.

Aftercare: To prevent the plants from becoming straggly and woody always trim them during July. Because rosemary can only produce new growth from one-year-old stems take care not to cut back into the old wood.

Harvesting: Cut fresh young shoots throughout the growing season. Excess shoots can be cut for drying.

Flavour: Pine/lemon.

Use: Mostly used with lamb dishes.

Sage – *Salvia officinalis*
Hardy evergreen perennial.

Height and spread: 60 cm (2 ft) × 90 cm (3 ft).

Site and soil: Full sun, good moisture-holding loam.

Propagation: Usually brought in as a pot-grown plant, can be propagated by heel cuttings taken during the summer. Grow on in a pot and plant out when large enough.

Aftercare: The branches are brittle and prone to splitting, but the damaged sections can be pegged into the ground then covered with soil to produce new roots.

Harvesting: Cut fresh leaves as required throughout the growing season. If some of the leaves are needed for drying, spread them out somewhere warm to dry for about a week and then store in an airtight container.

Flavour: Musty/smoky.

Use: Soups, stews.

Sweet cicely – *Myrrhis odoratus*
Hardy perennial.

Height and spread: 60–90 cm (2–3ft) each way.

Site and soil: Partial shade. Fertile, moist soil but free draining.

Propagation: Seed, sown in modules or directly into the soil. After planting out it will self-seed freely. The seedlings can be dug up and replanted as required. Plant out at 90-cm (3-ft) spacings all round.

Aftercare: Water in dry weather and remove any unwanted self-sown plants. If the leaves are cut regularly it will help to control the vigour of the plant. If the plants are left to their own devices they can reach a height of 150 cm (5 ft).

Harvesting: Harvest the leaves as soon as they fully grown. To maintain the leaf production remove any flowers just before they are about to open.

Flavour: The green leaves are aniseedy.

Use: The dried leaves can be used as a sweetener in fruit pies and desserts. The roots can be used in salads or as a boiled vegetable.

Tarragon – *Artemisia dranunculus*
Perennial.

French tarragon is the best culinary variety to use.

Height and spread: 90 cm (3 ft).

Site and soil: Full sun, with protection from cold winds. Good free-draining loam.

Propagation: Must be brought in as a pot-grown plant. Tarragon does not grow well from seed. It is best propagated from root division or cuttings taken during April/May.

Aftercare: Never allow the plants to dry out, but do not over-water. Move plants to a new site every four years. Protect from the worst of the winter weather.

Harvesting: Cut fresh leaves throughout the growing season. To dry take young shoots during late summer just before the flowers appear.

Flavour: Aniseedy/peppery.

Use: As a flavouring in wine vinegar and in Hollandaise sauce. Also used with chicken and egg dishes.

Thyme – *Thyhmus vulgaris*

Hardy evergreen perennial.

Height and spread: 25 cm (10 inches) × 30 cm (1 ft).

Site and soil: Full sun, free-draining loam.

Propagation: Usually from bought-in plants. Cuttings from young shoots can be taken during June and July and grown on until large enough to plant out.

Aftercare: Because thyme is a low-growing plant, keep the surrounding area weed free to prevent it from becoming smothered. Once established it does not need to be watered. Trim using garden shears after flowering.

Harvesting: Cut fresh young sprigs of shoots during the growing season. To dry, cut sprigs of leaves and place in a dark warm room.

Use: Rub onto meat before roasting. Often used in stuffings and as flavouring for stews.

3

fruit

In this chapter you will learn:
- how to grow soft fruit
- how to grow top fruit
- how to choose and plant fruit trees.

Growing fruit

Every gardener should set aside a part of their garden on which to grow some fruit trees or bushes, even if you only have enough room for a few plants in pots. Your rewards will be well worth the effort – fruit as you have never tasted it before.

Fruit has really been a victim of the modern lifestyle, with its one-stop shop approach to retailing. It is a living, breathing thing and possesses distinctive qualities that cannot be packaged and made presentable for the lines of shelves in the way that washing powder or canned soup can. Tragically, most of the fruit that is offered for sale today has been picked up to six weeks before it is ready to harvest and is then put into cold stores and 'ripened' artificially to make it ready for selling to the general public. The end result of all of this artificial manipulation of the fruit harvest is that the consumer has to accept a grossly inferior product that does not bear any resemblance to the true taste and texture of the real thing.

To be able to enjoy something as simple as a strawberry or as exotic as a peach can be your reward, with just a little bit of effort. The critical thing is to be able to pick the fruit when it is at the point of perfect ripeness, and this is the option that the home grower has when they are managing their own fruit plot.

It is often wrongly thought that fruit is difficult to cultivate. It is no more demanding than growing carrots or the perfect rose, but it has to be considered as a long-term investment and it may be several years before you can enjoy the fruits of your labours.

The secret is not to rush in and plant your favourite fruit trees or bushes without carrying out a little bit of research beforehand. The proverb 'Act in haste, repent at leisure' has never been more appropriate than where fruit growing is concerned. First of all, make a list of the varieties that you would like to grow. Next, you will have to check to find out if they are suitable for your soil, climate, region, and what other criteria will have to be taken into consideration before placing your order. This task is not as daunting as it may appear. Most of the information you require can be found quite easily just by looking in fruit catalogues. They contain a host of valuable information that will help to remove most of the mystery that surrounds fruit growing. The fruit nurserymen themselves will be only too pleased to answer your questions no matter how stupid they may seem to you. They love what they do for a living and share in your ambitions to grow fruit successfully. Listen to them, take their advice and you won't go far wrong.

It is possible to enjoy fresh fruit grown in the garden all the year round. The fruit season traditionally starts with the soft fruits, especially strawberries, that can be forced under glass to crop by late March to April, before the traditional strawberry season of May and June begins. Then there are late summer–autumn cultivars that will provide a harvest at the end of September into October. To keep up the supply there are red and white currants, gooseberries and blackcurrants to fill the months of June, July and August. Raspberries, available from June until October, must also be added to the list. And there are other summer soft fruits such as loganberries and blueberries that are worthy of consideration too.

Tree fruits ('top fruits') also make their contribution to this delicious and succulent harvest, starting with early apricots that are ripe by late June, followed by the later varieties that carry the season on into July and August. Peaches and nectarines also become available during July and August. Cherries must be added to the list for July and August, and plums are available from late July until the end of September. The earliest of the apples are ready to pick and eat straight from the tree during July, followed by the remainder of the early and late apples that take the season on into October. Pears have a similar season to apples but they cannot be stored for any great length of time. The last of the apples harvested are put into store and will keep right up until the early spring when the first of the forced strawberries are just ready for picking.

General guidelines

There are a few general rules to observe and success will follow:

- Fruit trees and bushes will not tolerate cold, waterlogged ground.
- Always check the pH of the soil. Strawberries prefer a slightly acid soil. The stone fruits will need a higher pH to grow well.
- Avoid trying to grow fruit trees and bushes in a frost trap.
- Select a sunny open site that is sheltered from strong winds.
- Dig over the entire fruit plot to improve the soil; do not plant in individual holes as these will only act as sumps, collecting water and leading to suffocation of the root system.

- There is no need to dig in manure. It will only promote soft, leafy growth that will be vulnerable to pest and disease attack. Only improve the soil if it is in poor condition, using a tree planting mix that can be bought from any garden centre.
- Buy in bare-rooted trees and bushes that are planted during the autumn; this gives the plants the best chance of surviving.
- If a tree requires the support of a stake, put the stake in the hole first, remembering to place it off centre so that the tree can go in the middle of the hole.
- Use tree guards to protect the trunk of the tree from being damaged by squirrels, rabbits, deer or machinery such as strimmers.

Fruit growing is divided into two types:

1 Soft fruit, which includes all of the plants and bushes that produce soft berries, such as strawberries and raspberries.
2 Top fruit, which includes all of the woody trees that produce fruits along the branches, such as apples and plums.

Before you begin your fruit growing, you must clear the fruit plot of all perennial weeds and dig it well, only adding organic matter to the soil if it is in poor condition. To avoid repetition, the rest of this chapter will assume that you have done this.

Soft fruit

General guidelines

Soft fruit grows best on soil with a pH of 6.0. If it is over 7.0 the leaves of the plants will become yellow between the veins. This is lime-induced chlorosis, caused by the calcium in the soil locking up the nutrients and making them unavailable to the plants. It can easily be remedied by spraying the foliage of the plants with Epsom salts. Chlorosis is often mistaken for a virus infection, but in the latter the veins are yellow and the leaf displays some green pigment. All of the soft fruits are every bit as attractive to birds, mice and squirrels as they are to us, so some form of net protection will need to be erected to cover the plants. It does not have to be an expensive fruit cage to be effective – netting supported on wooden stakes or canes will do the job just as well.

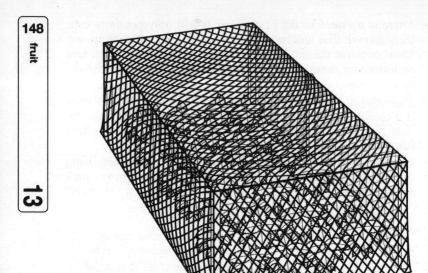

figure 13.1 netting strawberries

Always use certificated virus-free stock plants purchased from reputable growers (see the 'Useful contacts' list in 'Taking it further'). Avoid free gifts from friends and neighbours because quite innocently they could be giving you plants infected with a virus.

Blackcurrants

The blackcurrant season is from July/August to September. Blackcurrants have been the workhorse of the soft-fruit garden for many years. Red and white currants may have gone in and out of fashion but the blackcurrant has always survived. This is probably because it is packed with health-giving vitamin C and can be eaten uncooked or made into jams and preserves.

Planting

Plant from October to March except when the ground is frozen or waterlogged. Blackcurrants are grown as stooled bushes (roots or stumps from which shoots spring). To achieve this they are planted about 15 cm (6 inches) deeper in the soil than they were grown in the nursery, to encourage the production of underground shoots. These are not to be regarded as suckers. Blackcurrants can make quite big bushes, up to 1.8 m (6 ft) tall, so be prepared to give them plenty of room.

Distance between plants – 1.8 m (6 ft).

Distance between rows – at least 1.8 m (6 ft).

Cultivation

Blackcurrants make plenty of strong growth in a season. Top-dress around the plants using a general fertilizer in March, and at the same time apply a 5-cm (2-inch) deep mulch between the plants.

Pruning

Established bushes: Blackcurrants carry their fruit on the *previous* summer's growth. Pruning could not be simpler – just remove the old fruited branches. Ideally pruning should be carried out immediately after harvesting or, more practically, in September.

By the end of summer the blackcurrant bush will be a mass of fresh young shoots surrounding the older fruiting branches. The older wood that has produced the blackcurrants will have turned dark brown during the summer and needs to be cut right out at soil level just above a cluster of buds. This will leave a jungle of pale-green, one-year-old shoots that need to be organized. First cut out all of the weak, crossing and badly placed shoots. The next stage of the exercise is to select five to seven strong, evenly spaced upright shoots that will carry next year's crop. Everything else must be pruned down to soil level. A halo or crown of shoots should be the end result.

Newly planted bushes: The newly planted bushes must be pruned down to soil level at pruning time. This will allow the buds that are below the soil to grow and produce the shoots that will carry the first crop in the second summer after planting. The shoots that grow in the first summer *must not* be pruned – it is vital to understand that you will not get a crop in the first year but the shoots that have been grown are the ones that will carry the first crop. At the end of the second summer after planting, prune the bushes as described for established blackcurrants.

Propagation

Blackcurrants are easily propagated from hardwood cuttings that are taken in the autumn. They must be prepared from the current season's growth, and the best time to carry out this job is after the late summer pruning of the bushes has been completed. Select the cutting material from healthy young prunings that are about as thick as a pencil (6 mm/0.25 inches). Cut back the tip of the shoot by about 5 cm (2 inches) and make the cutting 30 cm (12 inches) long.

Little more is required to the preparation of the hardwood cutting, other than to strip all of the lower leaves off but leaving all of the buds intact. As mentioned earlier, blackcurrants are always grown as stooled bushes and the lower buds will develop into underground shoots. A slit trench is made in the soil, in which two-thirds of the length of the prepared cutting is buried. A 2.5-cm (1-inch) layer of horticultural grit can be spread over the bottom of the trench to improve rooting conditions if you have poorly draining soil. Lightly firm the soil around the cuttings using the heel of the boot. Water them in to settle the soil, and be prepared to protect them against freezing weather conditions. They will be rooted by next summer and ready for transplanting next autumn.

Redcurrants and white currants

The currant season is from June to August. The cultivation and management of red and white currants is identical to that of the gooseberry, which makes them an ideal partner in the soft-fruit garden. Both of them are easy to grow and have no major disease problems and, like the gooseberry, they can be long lived. The redcurrants will grow in shade, but under these conditions they do not have as much colour and flavour as when they are grown in full sun. However the tastes and uses of red and white currants are very different.

• Redcurrant fruits are seedy and they are generally used for making jellies and preserves that are served with game dishes.
• White currants are eaten as a dessert fruit. They are sweet and less seedy than their red cousins.

Both look stunning when used in combination with other summer fruits.

Gooseberries

The gooseberry season runs from June/July to August. It is the earliest of the outdoor soft fruits to be ready for harvesting. They flourish in cooler conditions and make long-lived plants. Normally they are grown on a single short leg as open-centred bushes, but where space is at a premium they can be trained as a fan shape or cordon. Gooseberries are tolerant of a wide range of soil types provided that they are not waterlogged or too free draining. The gooseberry flowers early in the spring, so it is essential to provide them with a sheltered site that will protect the flowers against frost damage. A sunny site is not essential – it is possible to grow gooseberries trained against a north-facing wall.

Planting

The planting season is from October to March whenever soil conditions permit. Do not plant into frozen or waterlogged ground. Check along the stems of the plants for dormant buds or small white shoots. These must be rubbed out to prevent them from growing and producing suckers. Plant with the roots just below the soil surface. Avoid planting too deeply because this will encourage root suckers to develop.

For bushes, espaliers or fans:

Distance between plants – 1.9 m (6 ft).
Distance between rows – 1.9 m (6 ft).

For single cordons:

Distance between plants – 45 cm (18 inches).
Distance between rows – 1.9 m (6 ft).

For multiple cordons allow 45 cm (18 inches) for each extra stem.

Support each of the stems of the cordons with a 1.8-m (6-ft) bamboo cane to train them along.

Cultivation

Gooseberries are hungry feeders. Top-dress around the bushes with a general fertilizer each March. They are very sensitive to any potash deficiency in the soil. This is indicated by the leaves of the plants turning brown around their edges. If the lack of potash is not dealt with the bushes will eventually stop producing gooseberries. If any plants display the symptoms, water around them with tomato fertilizer, which is high in potassium and should correct matters.

Avoid disturbing the soil to any depth around the root area. Gooseberries will produce suckers from any damaged roots as well as their stems. The suckers must be pulled off rather than cut, to prevent them re-growing. June and July are the best months to do this job because the suckers will still be soft at this time of the season.

The fruits will need thinning during May, and although the thinnings will be too sour to eat uncooked, they will make excellent pies and tarts. Thin out the fruits so that each individual berry has room to grow to its full size.

Pruning

New plants: The main objective of pruning young bushes is to create a 'goblet' shape on a single 45-cm (18-inch) long leg. Any badly placed or crossing shoots that are not making a contribution to the formation training are pruned out at the planting stage.

Prune back the shoots of newly planted bushes to 8 cm (3 inches) during March; prune to an upward-facing bud. There will be no harvest in this first season. The new growth will be used to form the future fruiting shoots. Over the next three seasons carry out summer and winter pruning as described above until the bush has filled its allocated space.

Established bush trained plants: The main objective of pruning here is to create and maintain an open-centred framework. This will allow light and airy conditions within the plant, which will greatly reduce the odds of later problems from pests and diseases. By opening up the centre of the bush it will also make picking a much less painful task.

Summer pruning: Gooseberries fruit on short laterals or spurs that grow from older wood or on shoots that are at least one year old. During late June and into July, prune back the laterals to about five leaves from the main stems to encourage the formation of fruit buds. Cut out any shoots that are likely to crowd the centre of the bush, especially any strong-growing shoots that will compete with the trained framework branches. Do not cut back the tips at this time as it is a winter job.

Winter pruning: Cut back the laterals that were summer pruned to 5 cm (2 inches), pruning just above a bud. At the same time cut back the young leader growth by half. Cut to an upward-facing bud to encourage vertical growth on lax cultivars (those with shoots that tend to curve downwards) and to an outward-facing bud on the upright types.

Propagation

Gooseberries are propagated from hardwood cuttings. The cuttings are prepared in almost the same way as those of blackcurrants; the main difference this time is that all of the spines and buds are removed up to within three buds from the top of the cutting. This is to produce a plant with a clear stem with no shoots growing from below the soil. The buds left at the top of the cutting will eventually be developed into the fruit-bearing branches.

Grapes – *Vitis vinifera*

Grapes are traditionally associated with grand vineries like the famous one at Hampton Court, but there are cultivars suitable for growing outdoors. However, the quality of the harvest will always be a problem in the UK.

The grape or vine originated in Asia Minor and its cultivation spread westward over the centuries as trading routes were opened up, and now it is grown all around the world. Vines need frost-free springs that are followed by warm, dry summers with plenty of sunshine hours. The winter temperatures should be cold enough to induce dormancy but not so cold as to damage or kill the vine. Growing grapes outdoors is difficult because the British climate cannot be relied upon to provide all of these requirements over a growing season. Growing outdoor vines is possible in the southern-most counties of the British Isles, anywhere under a line drawn across the country from London to Cardiff.

Raspberries

The raspberry season runs from late June to October. Raspberries grow well under cooler conditions and will suffer badly in the hotter summers. Ideally they like to have their roots in cool, moist shade and their heads in the light. Traditionally, raspberries are associated with the west of Scotland because of the ideal growing conditions that it can provide. On lighter, more free-draining soils that dry out quickly, raspberries will struggle unless plenty of organic, moisture-holding material is worked in to it. An annual mulch applied during March will also help to conserve moisture and keep the roots cool.

Planting

There are summer-fruiting and autumn-fruiting cultivars of raspberries. Both are planted at the same time but the methods of management are different.

The planting season is from late October to November while the soil still has enough warmth in it to encourage further root development and the air temperature is low enough to prevent the shoot buds from breaking into growth. Plant at a depth of 5 cm (2 inches). Make sure that the growth buds along the roots are below the surface of the soil to prevent them from drying out. Plant firmly and then cut the cane down to 15 cm (6 inches) above the soil.

Distance between plants – 45 cm (18 inches).
Distance between rows – 2 m (6 ft).

Cultivation

In March, top-dress along the rows with a general fertilizer, stirring it in with a hoe. At the same time, apply a mulch between the rows of canes, covering all of the soil area.

During the summer, hoe regularly between the rows to control any shoots that may be produced away from the main lines.

Pruning

Summer-fruiting raspberries bear fruit on the *previous* summer's growth. This means that the canes that are in the first summer will have to be tied in as explained below, but they will not be able to fruit until the following summer, after which they are treated as described.

Summer-fruiting types must be pruned soon after they have finished cropping. This can be done from late July until the end of September, depending on the cultivar. Cut away the ties holding the old fruiting canes to the supporting wires and then prune them down to soil level, leaving only the fresh young canes that have been produced during the current summer. Not all of the new canes will be required for the next year, so select the five best canes per plant, spacing them out evenly along the wire before tying them in.

During late February, tip back the canes to 1.9 m (6 ft) to induce more flower production along the canes.

Autumn-fruiting raspberries bear their fruit on the *current* season's growth. Prune them during February when the new season's shoots are just showing through the surface of the soil. Cut all of the previous season's growth down to soil level. It is difficult to control the growth of the autumn bearers because they tend to form a thicket and not grow in an orderly line. The canes cannot be tied to any form of support, but they can be enclosed within a fence of stakes and stout string. They are not pruned down at the end of the season but allowed to go into the winter still carrying all of the summer's canes. Hoe ruthlessly in between the rows to keep them free of suckers and do not allow the lines to creep out and thicken.

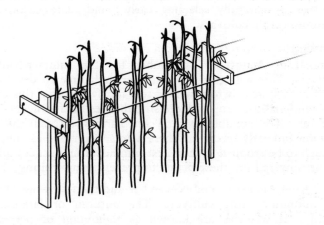

figure 13.2 supporting autumn-fruiting raspberries

Propagation

Raspberry plants usually remain productive for about 12 years, by which time they will have become heavily virused and unproductive. They will have to be dug up and burnt to prevent the risk of infecting any new plants. The soil will also have become infected with virus diseases, so under no circumstances be tempted to plant new canes on the old site. A brand new raspberry bed must be made.

Strawberries

Strawberries will grow best in a soil that is fertile and well drained but moisture holding. They will not tolerate shallow, thin soils that are liable to dry out quickly during periods of dry weather. The site must be sunny and free from shade. They like to feel the warmth of the sun on their faces.

After a while, strawberries will be attacked by viruses that are difficult to control. The leaves and fruits become pale and distorted, and the general appearance of the plants gives cause for concern. To avoid this it is always best to create a fresh strawberry patch every three years on another piece of the garden using brand new, virus-free plants. It is a false economy to propagate plants from your old stock. Make a clean start every time. The old plants can be quite safely put on the compost heap.

It is possible to spread the strawberry season from April to October by carefully selecting early-, mid-, late-season and autumn-bearing cultivars.

Planting

Plant from August to September for the summer-fruiting cultivars. This will give the plants enough time to develop a good root system before winter sets in. By planting this early you can harvest a crop of large strawberries the following June and July. It is possible to carry on planting through the late autumn and early spring but these plants will not be established enough to be cropped in their first summer. You must cut off all of the flowers from these plants to prevent them fruiting.

Plant from August to mid-November and the following March for autumn-fruiting cultivars. The autumn or late-season fruiting strawberries are known as *ramontant* or perpetual fruiting types. These extend the strawberry-picking season well into October. In the first year after planting, remove the early flush of flowers that are produced around May to allow further development of the plant during the summer. This will encourage the later production of strawberries during the autumn.

Planting directions: Plant firmly, with the crown or neck of the plant just level with the surface of the soil. If the crown is planted too deeply it could rot away and if it is set too high above the soil it will dry out and die. Just make sure that the soil has been gently firmed before any planting takes place to ensure that the newly planted crowns cannot sink into the soft soil.

Distance between plants – 45 cm (18 inches).
Distance between rows – 60 cm (2 ft).

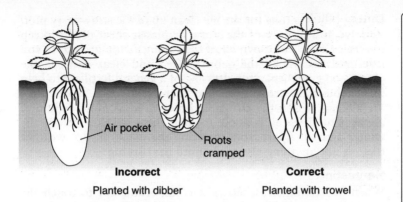

Incorrect

Planted with dibber

Correct

Planted with trowel

figure 13.3 planting strawberries

With strawberries growing so close to the ground they are always at risk of their flowers being damaged by spring frosts. To overcome this threat, try to grow them on the higher ground in the garden, to lift them out of the frost zone. It does not have to be a hillside – just 15 cm (6 inches) is sufficient. If your garden is entirely flat it may be worth considering making a raised bed to achieve the same effect.

> **Top tip**
>
> Avoid planting strawberries on the ground where potatoes, tomatoes, peppers and aubergines have been previously grown as the soil may have become infected with verticillium wilt.

Cultivation

Feed the strawberry bed with a top dressing of general fertilizer in early March to ensure development of strong, healthy plants. Open-ground plants will be flowering by May. Straw is used when the fruits are beginning to swell. It is tucked under the fruit trusses and foliage to keep the fruits clear of the ground, thus preventing them from being splashed with soil after rain or watering. The straw should be loose and also acts as a cushion, protecting the plants from any further damage during their development. The soil will absorb several degrees of frost, so delay putting straw or plastic underneath the plants until the last moment. Flowers that have been damaged by frost develop a black centre, which tells you that the embryo strawberry is useless.

During July it is time for the big clean up of the strawberry plot. Remove and dispose of the straw or plastic sheet used to keep the fruit clean. Cut down all of the summer's top growth to soil level and dispose of the debris. Weed and clear between the plants and give them a top dressing of a general fertilizer to help them rebuild the crowns for next year. Next year's flower buds are already within the crown and they need as much light and air around them as possible to help them develop before the winter arrives. Apart from watering the plants in dry weather there is not anything else to do until next spring.

Harvesting

When harvesting strawberries it is important not to touch the actual berry itself. They bruise very easily and after a few hours there will be bluish marks on the fruit where it has been damaged. Always pick strawberries by nipping through the stalk just behind the shoulders of the fruit. It can then be used as a carrying handle and the strawberry gently placed in a container lined with soft paper or cloth. To prevent crushing them, do not stack them more than two fruits high.

Never pick strawberries during the hottest part of the day. The fruits suffer in the heat and will be tasteless. Pick them in the early morning or evening and store somewhere cool. They will keep in good condition in the salad compartment of a refrigerator for about three or four days.

Propagation

During June and July the strawberry plants will begin to send out runners which, if left to their own devices, will quickly root and turn the strawberry bed into a tangled mess of unwanted extra plants and runners. These runners can be used to produce new plants, but if you do not need them for propagation purposes then cut them off close to the mother plant as soon as they appear.

Select only virus-free and healthy looking plants to propagate from. As the runner extends it will produce mini-strawberry plants along its length. Not all of these are required for propagation purposes. Using a staple made from soft garden wire, peg down the first plantlet produced into a 9-cm (3.5-inch) pot filled with potting compost. Cut off the runner beyond this point, half bury the pot among the strawberry plants and water it regularly to encourage root development. By the end of August the roots of the new plant will have filled the pot and it will be ready for potting on into a larger pot. To do this, cut through the runner to free the young plant from the mother plant, trim the runner to tidy it up and take the new strawberry plant to the potting bench. Knock the plant out of the smaller pot and pot it into a 15-cm (6-inch) pot containing potting compost. Water it in to settle the plant and place it in a cold frame or on the north side of a wall. Allow the plant to be exposed to all weather conditions right up until the turn of the year. At this stage, protect the plant from the cold and wet of winter weather. By March it will be ready to plant out in the open ground, but remember not to allow it to produce fruit in its first season.

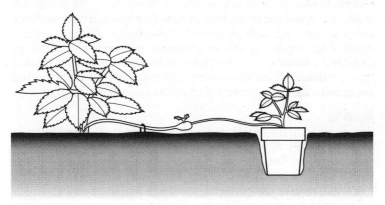

figure 13.4 propagating strawberries

Forcing strawberries into early production

There is a great deal of pride and satisfaction to be gained from being able to produce a dish of fresh, bright-red strawberries before they have even started growing in the open garden. It is quite easy to do this if you have access to frames or an unheated greenhouse. All you need are a few plants in pots that have been produced in the way described above. Bring them into the frame or greenhouse just before the end of the year. No artificial heat other than that produced by the sun shining through the glass is required. Early in the new year the potted plants will begin to grow. Ventilation must be given on hot days. By February the flower buds will begin to emerge and open. At this stage it will be necessary to hand-pollinate the flowers to be sure of a crop. As the strawberry fruits begin to swell, a little thinning is needed to remove any small or misshapen fruits and to limit the number of berries on each plant to about five or six. According to the weather conditions and light quality it is possible to pick strawberries by late March or April.

Another method of producing early strawberries is to cover a few plants in the garden with cloches during March. This will bring them forward by a month in advance of the unprotected plants.

Alpine strawberries

The alpine strawberry, sometimes known as fraise des bois, is closely related to the wild strawberry. It is the only member of the strawberry family that can be grown from seed. The plants are small, only growing to around 15 cm (6 inches) tall with no more than 30 cm (12 inches) spread. This makes them extremely suitable for modest spaces or container growing. The fruits are small but delicious and considered to be superior in taste to their larger cousins. We are all familiar with bright red strawberries but the alpine strawberry comes with white and yellow fruits as well.

Sowing

Sow from March to April under glass, maintaining a temperature of 20°C (68°F). Sow the seed in trays or pots filled with soilless seed compost. Don't cover the seed with compost until it has germinated. When it has, gently sieve seed compost through a fine mesh to give the emerging seedlings a light covering.

When the seedlings are large enough to handle prick them out singly into small pots or modules to grow on before planting them out in the open ground.

Planting

Plant from June to July. Choose somewhere shady where the soil is fertile and moisture retaining; avoid frost pockets. Plant out at 30-cm (12-inch) spacings, watering the plants well afterwards to settle them in. If the ground has a large water-holding capacity it is better to create a planting mound or ridge to improve the drainage conditions.

Allow for at least 30 cm (12 inches) of soil in each direction (length, width and depth) for each plant when growing the strawberries in pots or containers.

Harvesting

Harvest from June until the autumn frosts arrive. Pick over regularly to maintain berry production. The strawberry fruits can be cleaned by swirling them around in a dish of cold water.

Cultivation

Water the plants regularly, never allowing them to dry out. Heat stress or drought will bring flower and fruit production to a halt. When the top 25 mm (1 inch) of the soil shows signs of drying out it is time to give the plants a good soaking. To avoid problems with diseases don't water in the evening; it is safest to water early in the day so that the foliage can dry out. A mulch of organic material will help to conserve moisture and keep the roots cool.

Division

The alpine strawberry doesn't produce runners. Because is a perennial plant it can be dug up in the spring and cut up into three or four pieces. Replant them immediately.

Other hybrid berried fruits

For one reason or another these are the less commonly grown types of soft fruit. They all have their own individual characteristics that make them useful plants, but they can be demanding in their growing requirements. Most of them are the hybrid results of crosses that have been made between the various members of the berry and currant families.

Blackberry – *Rubus fruticosus*

The blackberry season runs from August to October. Although the wild blackberry has a much better flavour than the hybrid garden cultivars, do not be tempted to dig one up from the hedgerow and plant it in your garden. Wild varieties are extremely vigorous and will overrun the site during the course of one summer. Nowadays there are many cultivated forms of blackberries that have been specially bred to grow in gardens. Some are thornless, which makes picking much more pleasant; some are very vigorous growers and must be given plenty of room to grow. Most of the hybrid blackberry plants available today have been developed from American and European types of blackberries.

The American plants are vigorous and have more thorns than the European strains, and they fruit earlier than the European varieties. The berries are long and black and have a sharp flavour.

The European plants are also very vigorous, making them unsuitable for growing in small gardens, but some of the thornless cultivars are less vigorous. Both of them have the traditional wild blackberry flavour.

Planting

Before you do any planting out, you must erect a training system of posts and wires to tie and train the blackberry canes against. Set two stout end posts at least 5 m (16.5 ft) apart. The posts need to be firmly buried 60 cm (2 ft) in the ground, with 2 m (6 ft) above ground. Fix the lowest training wire 45 cm (18 inches) above the soil level, and add two more tiers of wires, one near the top of the post and the other in the middle. Plant the blackberry at the centre of the framework from October to November.

Distance between plants – 5 m (16.5 ft).
Distance between rows – 2 m (6 ft).

Pruning and training

Pruning new plants: Prune the canes as low down as possible. There will be no fruit in the first summer. The canes must be trained into position to crop in the second summer.

Pruning established plants: At the end of summer the older fruited wood has to be removed completely. During the summer, select about six fresh young new canes to tie along the lowest wire, to be tied in to replace the old canes.

Blackberries can easily produce shoots or rods that can be up to 4.5 m (15 ft) in length in one season. Do not shorten the new canes during the summer – you will have to tie them in before pruning them to fill the wires.

To sustain this amount of growth, top-dress around the plants and between the rows with a general fertilizer in March.

Blueberry – *Vaccinium corymbosum*

Most of the cultivated forms of blueberry that are to be found in gardens today are bred from the North American blueberry. There are two distinct types to be found in cultivation: the high bush that can reach a height of 1.5 m (5 ft) and the shorter-growing low bush that may grow to 60 cm (2 ft) tall. The dwarf varieties are especially suitable for growing in pots, raised beds or containers. Both varieties of blueberries require the same growing conditions. Their natural growing habitat is in boggy soil, which is very acidic with a pH of 5.5. Because most garden soils are not this acidic these conditions are difficult to replicate in the garden. Always carry out a pH test on the soil before buying any plants.

There are British and European forms of blueberries that grow wild on the acidic, heathland moors of mountains, but they are vastly inferior in taste to the cultivated forms.

Although blueberries are considered to be self-fertilizing, it is recommended to always plant two different cultivars to cross-fertilize each other and ensure that there is a good crop of berries.

Planting
Plant from late October to November, with a distance of 1.5 m (5 ft) each way between plants.

Cultivation
Mains water could contain lime or chemicals that will affect the growth of the bushes. Only water with rainwater. Mulch around the bushes with well-rotted wood chips or bark to conserve moisture and suppress weed growth.

Pruning
Very little pruning is required in the early years other than to cut out weak, crossing, damaged or diseased branches. After a few years some of the older wood will become less productive and will have to be pruned out, to be replaced by younger wood.

Boysenberry – *Rubus ursinus*
The boysenberry season runs from July to August. The boysenberry is believed to be the product of a cross between a loganberry, a blackberry and a raspberry, but the exact parentage is not known for certain. It is named after Rudolph Boysen, an American who has been credited with its introduction during the 1930s, and it certainly deserves to be more widely grown. It is similar to the loganberry but it better suited to growing on lighter free-draining soils. The long berries begin to turn red when ripening commences, finally ending up a deep purple colour.

Planting
As for raspberries, the planting season is from late October to November. Plant at a depth of 5 cm (2 inches).

Distance between plants – 4.5 m (15 ft).
Distance between rows – 1.9 m (6 ft).

Pruning and training

Cut out all of the fruited canes at the end of the summer and train the current season's canes to the supporting framework.

Cranberry – *Vaccinium macrocarpon*

The cranberry season is from September in the south of the UK to October in the north. The low-bush cranberry (not to be confused with the mountain cranberry, *Vaccinium vitis-idaea)* is a close relative of the blueberry.

Cranberries have quite specific growing requirements because they are descended from bog plants and need to be provided with an acid soil with a pH of 5.5. If your soil has a pH higher than this then you will have to construct a raised bed filled with an ericaceous compost to grow them on. It will be impossible to maintain the low pH simply by excavating a hole in the soil and filling it with ericaceous compost, because the leaching effect from the surrounding soil will always raise the pH level.

Cranberries are low-growing plants that produce upright fruiting shoots as they spread over the surface of the ground. They flower during the month of June and fruit during the late summer and early autumn.

Planting

Plant from late October to November, with a distance of 30 cm (1 ft) each way between plants. Mulch the bed with lime-free horticultural grit to prevent the compost from drying out.

Cultivation

Only use rainwater to water cranberry plants. The mains water in your area may have a pH that is too high for them. If you live in an area of high rainfall they will need less irrigation than in drier regions. Take care to ensure that the bed does not begin to dry out. Cranberries are moisture-loving plants and it is better to keep the beds wet but not sodden.

Pruning

Cut down the fruiting shoots after harvesting. Prune out any damaged upright shoots and any of the main spreading shoots that have been disturbed.

Prune established cranberry beds during the autumn. Thin out any overcrowded main shoots and upright shoots and, at the same time, trim the edges of the bed to keep it neat.

Jostaberry – *Rubus x culverwellii*

The jostaberry season runs from July to September. A cross between a blackberry and gooseberry hybrid with a blackcurrant and *R divaricaticum* hybrid, the jostaberry is considered to be superior to the Worcesterberry. The growth is upright and thornless. It is self-pollinating and produces fruits that look like very large blackcurrants. The flavour is pleasing but does not really taste of either blackcurrant or gooseberry. If you ever inherit a garden containing something that looks like a blackcurrant but you remain uncertain about its identity, it could be a jostaberry. Blackcurrants will give off a distinctive blackcurrant scent if their leaves are crushed, so if you crush a few leaves and there is no blackcurrant smell then it may be a jotsaberry!

Planting

Plant from late October to November at a depth of 5 cm (2 inches) and with a distance of 2 m (6 ft) all round; they can grow to a height of 1.8 m (6 ft).

Pruning

It will take a few seasons to build up the fruiting wood, so crops will be light at first. After leaf fall, prune out any weak or crossing branches. During June and July cut back any tall leading shoots to keep the plants under control and to encourage the formation of the next season's fruit buds. After a few years, some of the shoots will become woody and unproductive. Prune these out low down and replace them with the younger branches.

Loganberry – *Rubus x loganobaccus*

The loganberry season runs from July to August. Loganberries require a lot of room to grow – they can make up to 4 m (13 ft) of growth in a season. The original loganberry had thorns just like a blackberry, but the thornless cultivar L654 dominates the market these days.

Planting

As for raspberries, the planting season is from late October to November. Plant at a depth of 5 cm (2 inches). Make sure that the growth buds along the roots are below the surface of the soil to prevent them from drying out. Plant firmly and then cut the cane down to 15 cm (6 inches) above the soil.

Distance between plants – 5 m (16.5 ft).

Pruning

Pruning newly planted canes: Cut all of the canes down to soil level after planting. The new canes produced will not carry fruit in their first summer. They will crop in their second season. Tie the young canes to their supporting wires as they develop. In the second summer after planting, the plants will produce a fresh set of canes that have to be bundled together to replace the older fruiting wood.

Pruning and training established plants: Remove all of the fruiting canes at the end of summer. Tie in to the training wires the new young canes that will carry next season's crop.

Cultivation

Avoid breaking the roots by digging too deeply around the plants. Keep weeds under control by regular hoeing and mulching.

Tayberry – *Rubus loganobaccus 'Tayberry'*

Raised in Scotland, this thorned plant has a long cropping period from July to August. The fruit is sweeter and more aromatic than the loganberry. It is the result of a cross between a blackberry and a raspberry.

Plant 2.5 m (8 ft) apart. Early crops of medium sweet berries are good for jamming. They require the same cultivation as the raspberry.

Worcesterberry – *Ribes divericatum*

This is a distinct species. It is the product of a cross between a gooseberry and a blackcurrant. They make large bushes that are even thornier than a gooseberry, which makes picking very painful. The fruit resembles a gooseberry and tastes vaguely like a blackcurrant.

Plant from October to November, allowing 2 m (6 ft) each way between plants. Mulch around the plants to retain moisture and control weeds. To prevent suckering, avoid digging too deeply around the roots of the plants.

Top fruit

Planting any type of fruit tree requires you to make a long-term commitment – it can occupy the site for up to 40 years and you may have to wait two or three years before you can harvest your first fruits. There are several things that have to be taken into consideration before rushing out and buying a fruit tree for your garden. The following information aims help you make your final choice.

Top fruit includes apples, pears, plums, cherries, peaches, apricots and nectarines. These can either be grown as standard trees, formally trained espaliers, cordons or fans that can look attractive and be grown where space is at a premium.

An espalier is a horizontally trained branch. Usually espaliers are created in tiers or layers. A cordon is a tree that is planted at an angle of 45 degrees. It produces short fruiting branches along the trunk. A fan is a series of branches that radiate like the fingers of a hand from around 60 cm (2 ft) above soil level (see page 170 for examples).

Siting your fruit trees

Climatic considerations

Fruit trees are very demanding in their requirements and it has to be appreciated that they will not grow very well in some regions. The main criteria are altitude, rainfall, site, aspect, hours of sunshine, and protection from wind and frost. To a lesser degree the geographical location will have some influence as well.

- Any site that is more than 180 m (600 ft) above sea level is unsuitable for growing quality fruit, except perhaps for some of the more hardy culinary cultivars.
- A south-facing slope is always the first choice, with a western aspect the second.
- A site that is part way up a hillside is better than one lower down because cold air and frost will always drain down the slope to settle at the valley floor. Also, any site that is exposed to cold, searing winds will cause damage to flowers and foliage. A windbreak is a consideration, but they are an extra cost and it may not be practical to grow or erect one.
- Trees grown on sites near the sea risk suffering from salt-laden air, especially during high winds, although these areas do have the advantage of generally being frost free.

- The warmer western areas with their higher rainfall will provide the ideal breeding ground for diseases, such as canker and scab, to flourish. Quality fruit needs to be grown in areas that have a relatively modest level of rainfall of around 60 cm (24 inches) each season. There are trees that display some tolerance to these diseases but it does limit the ultimate selection.
- Plenty of sunshine and warmth are essential to the production of first-class dessert fruit. Apples are more tolerant of cold conditions than pears, cherries and plums. Apricots, peaches and nectarines will need the protection of south- or west-facing walls to grow well outdoors.

The biggest threat to fruit growing comes from late May frosts which can damage the developing fruit buds. A particularly heavy frost around blossom time could destroy the entire season's harvest overnight.

Soil

All fruit trees appreciate a fertile and free-draining loamy soil if they are to grow well and flourish. When they are planted in cold, wet soils the trees will be caught up in a continual struggle to survive and the fruit yield will always be poor. If the site has serious waterlogging problems that cannot be cured by improving the drainage, then it is better to reconsider your decision and find somewhere else to grow your fruit trees.

On the other hand, soil that is too free draining will present a totally different set of problems. These soils have no water-holding capacity at all and so they are always low in nutrients, which are washed out of the soil. However, it is relatively easy to cure these problems by digging in plenty of organic matter before planting. It does not have to be manure or garden compost, just as long as it improves the water-holding capacity of the soil.

A shallow soil overlying chalk will pose another set of difficulties, because the high pH will interfere with the tree's ability to take up nutrients. The solid layer of chalk will have to be broken up and the surrounding area improved before any planting can take place.

To sum up

The ideal site for growing fruit trees is sheltered from frosts and cold winds. It should be sunny, warm and well away from any overhanging shade from other trees or buildings. The soil should be a deep fertile loam with a pH that is slightly above neutral. Good drainage is essential to encourage strong, disease-free growth. This, of course, is the counsel of perfection, but the more that you can recreate these conditions the greater your chances of success will be.

Pollination

Nearly all fruit trees are self-sterile, which means that when a tree is flowering it cannot be fertilized by its own flower pollen. Fertilization can only be achieved by the successful transfer of pollen (cross-pollination) from another suitable tree growing nearby and is in flower at the same time. It does not have to be the same cultivar of fruit. To simplify this complicated process, fruit trees have been divided into groups according to their flowering periods and the trick is to plant two different cultivars together so that the flowers of one tree will pollinate the flowers of the other. The flowering groups have been given numbers to identify them and all you need to do is ensure that the type of tree you want to grow is always accompanied by its pollinator.

The various apple trees will produce flowers over a period from mid-April until the end of May. The pollination groups are: Group 1 – very early; Group 2 – early; Group 3 – mid-season; Group 4 – mid-season; Group 5 – late; Group 6 – late; Group 7 – very late. All of the information that you will need about this subject is contained within the catalogue description of the tree. If you have any doubts at all, contact the nursery, who will be only too happy to advise and guide you in your tree selection.

The shape of the tree

A fruit tree does not have to be grown in a lollipop shape on top of a 1.8-m (6-ft) trunk. In the walled kitchen gardens of the 1800s they were trained as fans, espaliers, cordons, pyramids and any other shape that took the head gardener's fancy. The one thing they did not have access to then was the range of rootstocks that we have available to us today. These allow us to grow trees that ordinarily would be too large for most gardens, and also to control their vigour and keep them well within bounds. In a small garden a tree could be trained flat against a wall or fence to form a decorative feature while also adding structure. Alternatively, it could be used to divide the garden up into compartments. Apples and pears can be trained to almost any shape you want, but the members of the stone fruit family are mainly suited to training as fans and are too vigorous to be grown where space is limited.

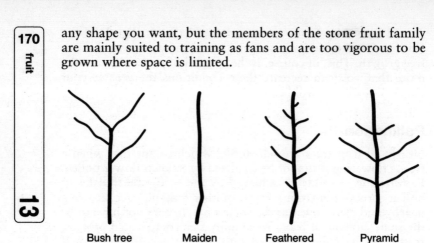

Bush tree   Maiden   Feathered maiden   Pyramid

Half standard or standard   Fan-trained   Espalier   Cordon

figure 13.5 fruit tree shapes

Buying your tree

It is well worth taking the time to carry out a little research before rushing out and buying your fruit trees. The fruit tree catalogues and websites are packed full of all sorts of helpful information that will guide you through the technical details that sometimes accompany the descriptions of each variety. Place your order well before the end of July to be certain of getting your first choice. The nurseries will only grow a limited number of trees and it is always first come, first served.

The main points to consider are:

- Variety of tree – make sure that it is suitable for growing in your area.
- Suitable pollinators – to ensure you get a reliable crop each year.
- Selection of rootstock – this will control the height and spread of the tree.
- Training of tree – what shape do you want: standard, cordon, bush?
- Age of tree – this is critical to the eventual training of the tree.

The best way to buy fruit trees is as bare-rooted, one-year-old maidens. They are able to withstand the shock of transplantation much better than older trees and they are at the perfect stage of development to be trained into any form you wish. A one-year-old maiden will have been lifted at the end of its first full season of growth and will look like a thin stick with roots on. There should not be any side branches, only dormant buds along the trunk. It is possible to purchase older trees that will have been trained already, but they will be more expensive.

The nursery will wrap and pack your trees well enough to survive a few days out of the ground, but you must unpack them as soon as possible after you have taken delivery of them. You will find them tied up in a tight bundle; do not bother to untie them at this stage, just plunge the roots in a bucket of water overnight to refresh them after their travails. Do not worry if, for some reason, you cannot plant the trees straight away, they can be heeled in on a spare piece of ground until they are required for planting.

It is possible to buy container-grown fruit trees, but these are not really worth considering because the development of the root system is disproportionate to the top growth and they will never develop into first-class trees.

Planting your tree

The best time to plant bare-rooted fruit trees is during their dormant season, which is from November until the middle of March at the latest. November to early December is the ideal time for planting because the soil is still warm enough to encourage the tree to make new roots before the onset of winter.

There are a few of points that are worth remembering when planting any tree, bush or shrub:

- Always make the hole at least 15 cm (6 inches) wider all round than the spread of the root system. Never cramp or twist the roots around to fit into too small a hole.
- Always take care to replant the tree to the depth at which it was originally grown in the nursery. This is indicated by a dark stain on the trunk of the tree, visible just above the roots.
- Finally, never bury the graft union as this will cause the tree to die. It can be found as a small swelling on the lower trunk of the tree.

It is always best to dig out the planting hole in advance of unpacking the tree or removing it from the heeling-in bed. The roots will dry out quite quickly. To stop this happening, cover them with damp hessian sacking or put them inside a plastic potting compost bag. At the planting stage any damaged roots can be cut back to healthy wood, but do not get carried away and cut off too much root.

Make sure the hole is wider than the root spread. When you are in the process of excavating the hole, put the soil from the top spit to one side and the soil from the lower spit to the other side of the hole: do not be tempted to mix them together. The soil at the bottom of the hole should be loosened but not turned over. This is to improve the drainage and allow the young developing roots to grow down into the soil.

All young trees need the support of a stake during the early years of their life. It is important to remember that it is the tree that is planted at the centre of the hole – the stake is always positioned on the windward side of the tree so that the prevailing wind will blow the tree away from the stake and not on to it.

- Place the tree at the centre of the hole and mark the position of the stake.
- Remove the tree and replace it in the protective sack.
- Drive the stake into the hole to a depth of about 45 cm (18 inches), taking care to keep it upright.
- Return the tree to the hole, carefully radiating the roots out within the hole, and then gently begin to cover the roots with the excavated topsoil a couple of centimetres at a time. Gently jiggle the tree up and down to settle the soil around the roots, to avoid air pockets.

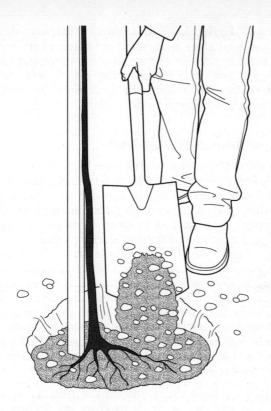

figure 13.6 planting out a fruit tree

- When the hole is half-filled with soil, lightly firm the soil around the roots using the heel of the boot.
- Continue to fill up the hole, using the soil from the lower spit only after all of the topsoil has been used up. When the soil is level with the surrounding area, lightly firm once more and secure the tree to the stake using a proper tree tie. Do not use string or wire – you will almost certainly garrotte the tree.
- Finally, soak the roots with 10 litres (2 gallons) of water and mulch around the tree, keeping the mulching material at least 15 cm (6 inches) away from the trunk.

Check regularly all through the winter to make sure that the tree is not loosened by frosts, and be sure to water it regularly all through the following summer.

Fruit trees will develop large root systems that, over the years, will grow out well away from the main trunk of the tree. The roots will begin to provide competition for water and nutrients when they are grown alongside other plants, and any deep cultivation of the soil around the trees must be avoided to prevent causing any damage to the roots.

The production of a fruit tree

Fruit trees grow erratically on their own roots. They can either be over vigorous, producing large and unmanageable trees, or too weak and spindly to be of any use to the grower. To overcome this, all fruit trees are produced in two parts that are grafted together (just like rose bushes). These are the rootstock and the scion (or the named variety of fruit chosen to be grown, e.g. apple, 'Bramley'). The rootstocks have been specially developed over many decades at fruit research stations, such as East Malling in Kent, where the rootstocks have been given the prefix 'M', or 'MM' in the case of apples. The scions are grafted or budded on to the rootstocks during the spring and summer and are allowed to grow on for one year before being offered for sale. Modern fruit trees of all kinds can now be produced on a wide range of rootstocks that allow gardeners to grow almost any kind of fruit tree they want to, within reason.

The rootstock controls the vigour of the tree, so a vigorous variety of fruit tree can be made to grow less vigorously and weak, disease-prone trees can be made to grow more strongly on an appropriate rootstock. The correct selection of rootstock can also allow fruit trees to be grown on a wide range of soil types that would otherwise be considered to be unsuitable for fruit production. The correct choice of rootstock can influence the time from planting to harvesting of the first fruits. There are some fruit trees that are slow to produce fruiting wood and these can be brought into bearing much earlier.

Top tip
Always thin apples down to one fruit per spur. Don't carry out this operation until after the 'June drop'.

There follows a brief description of the various types of fruit trees and the choices of rootstocks on which they are available.

Apples – *Malus domestica*
M27, extremely dwarfing, 1.8 m (6 ft) tall, spread 1.5 m (5 ft)

This rootstock produces a tree that will only be 1.8 m (6 ft) tall after 15 years. This makes it an excellent choice for growing in pots and other containers. Trees grown on M27 will require a stake or some form of support for all of their growing lives. This rootstock needs to be grown in a good fertile soil with regular watering and feeding.

Uses – dwarf pyramids, centre leader, stepovers/single tier espaliers.

Planting to maximum – cropping 2 years, average yield 7 kg (15 lbs).

Distance between trees – 1.5 m (5 ft).
Distance between rows – 1.8 m (6 ft).

M9, very dwarfing, 2.5 m (8 ft) to 3 m (10 ft) tall, spread 3 m (10 ft)

The standard dwarfing rootstock, but trees grown on M9 will need permanent staking. It is very versatile and is a good choice for producing small bush or pyramid trees, cordons and espaliers. It also requires a good fertile soil with regular watering and feeding. Well suited to the smaller garden.

Uses – bush, pyramids, centre leader, cordons.

Planting to maximum cropping – 2–3 years, average yield 20 kg (40 lbs).

Distance between trees – 3 m (10 ft).
Distance between rows – 4 m (13 ft).

M26, semi-dwarfing, 3.5 m (11.5 ft) to 4 m (13 ft) tall, spread 4 m (13 ft)

This rootstock is very similar to M9 but it produces more vigorous trees that are stronger growing. Because of this, staking is only required for the first five years of the tree's life. It performs well on average soils and the tree grown on M26 yield more fruit than M9.

Uses – bush, pyramids, centre leader, cordons, minarets, espaliers, containers and pots.

Planting to maximum cropping – 2–3 years, average yield 30 kg (65 lbs).

Distance between trees – 4 m (13 ft).
Distance between rows – 5 m (16.5 ft).

M106, semi-dwarfing, 4.4 m (15 ft) to 6 m (20 ft) tall, spread 5 m (16.5 ft)

One of the most suitable rootstocks available to the gardener, this will allow good crops to be produced under a wide range of growing conditions. Trees grown on MM106 will not require any staking after the first five years of their lives.

Uses – half standard trees, bush, espaliers, cordons, containers and pots.

Planting to maximum cropping – 3–4 years, average yield 45 kg (99 lbs).

Distance between trees – 4 m (13 ft).
Distance between rows – 5 m (16.5 ft).

MM111 and M2, vigorous, 6 m (20 ft) to 8 m (26 ft) tall, spread 5 m (16.5 ft)

This rootstock is much too vigorous for ordinary garden use. It produces trees that are far too tall and spreading. It is better suited to commercial orchards.

Uses – full standard trees.

Planting to cropping – 4–5 years, average yield 150 kg (330 lb).

Distance between trees – 5 m (16.5 ft).
Distance between rows – 6.5 m (22 ft).

M25, very vigorous, 5 m (16.5 ft) to 6 m (20 ft) tall, spread 6.5 m (22 ft)

Although this rootstock will perform well on a wide range of soil types, it is more suited to orchard work because it produces wide-spreading trees that are too big for the average garden. It may be worth considering if you have a very thin or sandy type of soil.

Uses – full standard trees.

Planting to cropping – 5–6 years, average yield 150 kg (330 lb).

Distance between trees – 6.5 m (22 ft).
Distance between rows – 8 m (26 ft).

> **Top tip**
> Always store apples with the stalk facing downwards.

Pears

Quince A, semi-dwarfing, 3.5 m (11.5 ft) to 6.5 m (22 ft) tall, spread 3.5 m (11.5 ft)

This is the most popular and commonly used rootstock for pears. It will produce healthy, productive trees on a wide range of soil types.

Uses – half standard tree, bush, pot or container, espalier, cordon.

Planting to maximum cropping – 4–5 years.

Distance between trees – 3.5 m (11.5 ft).
Distance between rows – 4.5 m (15 ft).

Quince C, dwarfing, 2.5 m (8 ft) to 3.5 m (11.5 ft) tall, spread 3.5 m (11.5 ft)

Has a little more dwarfing influence over the tree than Quince A, but it requires a highly fertile soil to perform well. Pear trees grown on this rootstock will require staking permanently.

Uses – bush, pyramid, central leader, espalier, cordon.

Planting to maximum cropping – 3–4 years.

Distance between trees – 3.5 m (11.5 ft).

EMH, dwarfing, 3.5 m (11.5 ft) tall, spread 4 m (13 ft)

A rootstock that produces trees that are between Quince A and C in vigour and that gives higher yields of larger pears. Trees grown on this rootstock will require staking for their first five years.

Uses – half standard, bush.

Planting to maximum cropping – 4–5 years.

Distance between trees – 4 m (13 ft).
Distance between rows – 5 m (16.5 ft).

Plums, including gages and damsons
St. Julien A, semi-vigorous, 6.5 m (22 ft) tall, spread 5 m (16.5 ft)

The standard rootstock used on all types of plum trees. It produces trees that will grow much too large for the average garden. One way of growing a plum tree in a small area is to train it against a wall as a fan-shaped tree. Plums are not suitable for very formal training as espaliers.

Uses – half standard tree, bush, walled-trained fan.

Planting to maximum cropping – 4–5 years.

Distance between trees – 5 m (16.5 ft).
Distance between rows – 6 m (20 ft).

Pixy, dwarfing, 2.5 m (8 ft) tall, spread 3 m (10 ft)

This rootstock can only be used on good fertile soils and trees grown on it must be well watered in dry conditions.

Uses – bush, pyramid, small fan, containers and pots.

Planting to maximum cropping – 3 years.

Distance between trees – 3 m (10 ft).
Distance between rows – 4 m (13 ft).

Cherries – sweet and acid
Colt, semi-vigorous, 4 m (13 ft) to 5 m (16.5 ft) tall, spread 5 m (16.5 ft)

The most common rootstock used for cherries. It is reliable on all types of land including poor soils. Stake trees for the first three years after planting.

Uses – half standard tree, bush, walled-trained fan.

Planting to maximum cropping – 4–5 years.

Distance between trees – 5 m (16.5 ft).
Distance between rows – 6.5 m (22 ft).

Gisela 5, semi-dwarfing, 1.8 m (6 ft) to 3.5 m (11.5 ft) tall, spread 3.5 m (11.5 ft)

This rootstock must to be grown in good, weed-free fertile soil. Chemical weed control around young trees must be avoided because it is sensitive to Glyphosate and other similar systemic herbicides. Trees must be staked for their first five years.

Uses – bush, small fan, containers and pots.

Planting to maximum cropping – 3 years.

Distance between trees – 3.5 m (11.5 ft).
Distance between rows – 4 m (13 ft).

Apricots, Peaches and Nectarines
St. Julien A, semi-vigorous, 5 m (16.5 ft) tall, spread 4 m (13 ft)

All three perform excellently on this tried and tested rootstock that has been used for many years. It performs well on poor soils and with orchard trees grown in grassland. The trees must be staked for the first three years.

Uses – standard tree, half standard tree, bush, walled-trained fan, container or pot.

Planting to maximum cropping – 4–5 years.

Distance between trees – 5 m (16.5 ft).

Distance between rows – 5 m (16.5 ft).

Pixy, dwarfing, 3 m (10 ft) tall, spread 3 m (10 ft)

This rootstock produces smaller and weaker trees. It can be used for pot work, but the trees will need to be grown in a rich compost with regular feeding and watering. Trees grown on Pixy come into fruiting earlier than on St. Julien but the overall yield is smaller.

Uses – bush, pyramid, small fan, container and pot.

Planting to maximum cropping – 3 years.

Distance between trees – 3 m (10 ft).
Distance between rows – 4 m (13 ft).

Top tip

Place a pad of cotton wool at the base of top fruit trees to attract and trap ants. They will crawl inside the pad seeking darkness.

Other fruiting trees

Citrus – *Citrus cvs.*

All members of the citrus family are best grown in pots. They should be outside during the summer but, because they will not survive outdoors during the winter, they should be brought in under glass during August. Citrus cannot cope with sudden changes of temperature very well, although they will tolerate temperatures as low as 5°C (40°F), but ventilation should be given on sunny days. Because citrus plants will flower and carry fruits all the year round, they have to be fed weekly during the summer and winter, using specific summer and winter soluble fertilizers. The fruits can take months to ripen and are usually ready for picking during the winter.

Figs – *Ficus carica*

There are figs that are hardy enough to grow outdoors in the British climate, but they will need careful management to encourage them to crop regularly. The fig needs a warm, sheltered site to grow well; it may be necessary to protect it with a layer of horticultural fleece in colder parts of the country. Figs produce two crops a season and this is what confuses most gardeners because at the end of summer there are large and small figs carried on the plants. The large figs have to be removed because they will not survive the winter. Leave any fig that is about as large as the tip of your little finger as these will overwinter and begin to swell the following summer. Water and feed the fig plants regularly while they are in full growth. Figs left to their own devices will grow into large trees. To control their vigour and force them into producing fruits they are usually planted in lined pits to restrict their root system. This makes them perfectly suited for growing in large pots

Medlars – *Mespiis germanica*

Medlars will grow anywhere on any type of soil provided that it is not waterlogged. The unusual hollow-shaped fruits are an acquired taste and are best served as a jelly preserve. They are best harvested during November after being exposed to a couple of frosts. The frosting will help to soften the fruit, which makes it easier to prepare. After the fruit has been picked it is left for a few weeks to begin to rot. This process is known as 'bletting'. If the medlars are not used by the end of December they will quickly decompose, becoming useless.

Mulberries – *Morus nigra*

Mulberries are long lived and grow into large gnarled trees with distinctive heart-shaped leaves. The highly edible fruits resemble large black raspberries and are carried during mid- to late summer. They were introduced into Britain by King Charles II to cultivate silk worms for the fledgling silk industry that he was hoping to establish. He was given the wrong information and bought the black mulberry (*M. nigra*) rather than the white mulberry *Morus alba* which silk worms live on.

Olives – *Olea europea*

Olives require a lot of warmth to produce first-class fruit. They will grow well in Britain, but because they will never ripen, they are best treated as an ornamental evergreen shrub. They will not tolerate hard frosts or cold, wet winter weather and need to be grown in pots to be brought in for the winter.

Quinces – *Cydonia oblonga*

The quince has long been used as a rootstock for pears, but it is a useful fruit in its own right. The pear-like fruits do not ripen until October and they are used mainly for making jams and jellies. Just like the pear, the quince will not tolerate cold winds, which makes it difficult to grow in all but the southern areas of the British Isles. After picking, keep the fruit well away from any apples and pears in store because the strong scent of the quince will taint them. Quinces are not suitable for small gardens because they will grow into very large trees.

Fruit harvesting chart

Soft fruit	Jan	Feb	Mar	Apr	May	June	July	Aug	Sept	Oct	Nov	Dec
Gooseberry					Thin	Pick	Pick					
Red currant						Pick	Pick					
White currant						Pick	Pick					
Blackcurrant						Pick	Pick	Pick	Pick			
Strawberry			Force	Force	Force	Pick	Pick	Pick	Pick	Pick		
Top fruit												
Apple	From store	From store					Pick and use	Pick and use	Pick and use	Pick and store	From store	From store
Pear							Pick	Pick	Pick	Pick	From store	From store
Cherry							Pick	Pick	Pick			
Peach							Pick	Pick	Pick			
Apricot						Pick	Pick					
Nectarine								Pick				
Plum							Pick	Pick	Pick			

calendar of work

JANUARY

Prune and clean vines and vinery.
Check and replace damaged labels.
Continue with winter digging.
Sow seeds of early crops.
Set up strawberry plants for forcing.
Pot on cuttings.
Prune fruit trees.
Protect overwintering crops.

FEBRUARY

Prick out seedlings; continue to sow seeds.
Continue with winter digging.
Plant out garlic and shallots towards the middle of the month.
Try and complete the winter pruning of fruit trees.
Spread organic matter over the root run of fruit trees.
Feed all fruit trees and bushes.

MARCH

Complete any outstanding planting and pruning.
Complete any unfinished soil preparation.
Continue seed sowing and pricking out.
Sow the first of the early crops outside.
Plant early tomatoes under glass.
Plant out first early potatoes.
Hoe at every opportunity.

APRIL

Continue with seed sowing, especially outdoors. Sow courgettes under glass.

Set up runner bean supports.

Continue to plant out potatoes in their cropping order.

Harvest the first of the early crops.

Continue to transplant earlier-sown crops.

Keep the hoe on the move.

Support peas as soon as they begin to grow.

Damp down the greenhouse on sunny days.

MAY

Earth up early potatoes.

Cut asparagus regularly.

Plant out April-raised runner beans or sow seed outdoors.

Begin to tie in and train growth of formally trained fruit trees.

Side-shoot tomatoes and tie to supports.

Sow early French beans under glass to transplant next month.

Irrigate if necessary.

Keep hoeing.

Damp down and ventilate the greenhouse.

JUNE

Continue to harvest crops regularly. This will maintain a steady supply.

Begin to lift early potatoes and continue with earthing up.

Harvest asparagus but stop cutting by the end of the month. Then give it a top dressing of general fertilizer to help it recover and build up for next year.

Harvest the first of the soft fruits.

Water the developing rows of peas.

Do not allow plants under glass to dry out or overheat.

Plant out courgettes after the fear of a late frost has gone.

JULY

Lift potatoes and carry on earthing up.

Begin to harvest the main crop of strawberries.

Harvest garlic and shallots after foliage turns yellow.

Keep up with harvesting of all crops now the garden is in full production.

Irrigate if necessary.

Begin to harvest the first of the orchard fruits.

Sow the overwintering crops of chicory and radicchios.

Plant out the last of the marrows, courgettes and pumpkins.

Pick tomatoes.

AUGUST

Continue with the harvesting of all crops.

Start to thin top fruit.

Delay any summer pruning of fruit trees until the end of the month. Start with the pears, then move on to apples. It is definitely the last chance to prune stone fruits.

Make the last of the outdoor sowing to provide a harvest for this season.

Lift onions towards the end of the month to put into store.

Trim any box hedging before the first of the frosts.

Harvest the earliest grapes.

SEPTEMBER

Complete the summer pruning of fruit trees and bushes.

Continue to harvest and put crops into store.

Try and lift the potatoes by the end of the month before the autumn rains arrive.

Harvest apples and pears to put into store.

Train and tie in fruit trees.

Select plants to provide seeds for next season.

Feed all late crops.

OCTOBER

Complete the harvesting of late crops, selecting only the best to put into store.

Clear ground of spent plants and sow a green manure.

Open up a trench for next season's runner beans.

Harvest the last of the tomatoes and remove them from the greenhouse.

Cut down summer-fruiting raspberries and burn the old canes.

Sow the last of the overwintering crops.

NOVEMBER

Begin winter digging.

Start to lift leeks and parsnips.

Collect and stack leaves to make leaf mould.

Prepare vegetables such as chicory for forcing.

Continue to control weeds.

Begin winter pruning of fruit trees and bushes.

Check that greenhouse heaters are working.

DECEMBER

Keep up with the winter digging.

Plant bare-root fruit trees and bushes, heeling in any that have to wait a while before planting.

Continue with winter pruning.

Check all tree ties and supports before winter sets in.

Protect overwintering crops.

Order seeds at the earliest possible time.

glossary

acid soil Soil that has a pH of less than 7.

aeration The replacement of stagnant soil air with fresh air.

alkaline soil Soil that has a pH of more than 7.

annual A plant that germinates, flowers and sets seed in one growing season, e.g. pea.

artificial fertilizer A chemical fertilizer of non-organic origin that is industrially manufactured. Sometimes referred to as 'straight fertilizers' because they supply one main nutrient for a crop; they can be combined to form a balanced feed, when they are called 'compound fertilizers'.

axil The angle formed between a leaf or a shoot and the main stem or branch of a plant.

balanced fertilizer Contains the three nutrients in the correct proportions for a given crop, e.g. potatoes.

base dressing An application of fertilizer that is incorporated into the soil before a crop is sown or transplanted.

biennial A plant that requires two growing seasons to complete its life cycle, e.g. onion, carrot.

biological control The use of natural predators to control pests; most commonly carried out in the greenhouse but can also be used outdoors.

blanching Growing vegetables in total darkness to produce tender succulent shoots, e.g. rhubarb, sea kale, Witloof chicory.

bolting The premature production of the seed head before the plant is mature, usually caused through stress at some time in its development, e.g. cold, heat, drought.

brassica Any member of the cabbage family, e.g. radish, turnip, Brussels sprouts, many of the Oriental vegetables.

broadcast To throw seed all over the soil surface instead of in rows.

cap The crust formed on the soil's surface through compaction.

catch cropping Sowing or growing a fast-maturing crop on a piece of ground before the site is required for a longer-growing main crop, e.g. early lettuce grown before planting up the site with Brussels sprouts.

chitting The practice of placing potatoes with the young bud shoots (the rose end) facing up towards the light to produce short green shoots. It can also include the pre-germination of seeds that are difficult to germinate before sowing in the open ground, e.g. beetroot, parsnip. The seed is placed in a container on damp paper or cloth overnight to swell.

chlorosis The yellowing of leaves caused by a mineral deficiency of the soil. The leaves lose their green colour between the veins but the veins remain green. This is more of a problem in soils with a high pH because they 'lock up' the nutrients, making them unavailable to the plants.

clamp A means of storing root vegetables through the winter. It is a soil mound that is lined with straw to protect the vegetables from the winter rains and frosts.

cloche A low-level glass or plastic tunnel that is placed over a crop to protect it from bad weather. It can also be used as a mini-greenhouse to allow the early sowing or transplanting of crops to make an early start in the late winter and spring.

companion planting The growing of a secondary crop that provides some form of protection for the main crop. It acts as an attractant to beneficial insects that will control attacks by insect pests to the main crop, e.g. tagetes are planted around plants such as tomatoes to control white fly.

complete fertilizer This contains the three main plant nutrients, N-P-K.

compost, garden Vegetable material decomposed through the action of bacteria. It is in a humified state and should be dark in colour and fibrous in texture.

compost, potting A specially mixed compost used in the growing on of plants in pots, trays and containers. It contains a mixture of loam/peat/coir, sand/vermiculite and a balanced supply of nutrients. It is not to be confused with garden compost.

compound fertilizer One that supplies more than one of the plant nutrients.

cordon A fruit tree or soft-fruit bush that is grown on a single main stem. The cordon is the main trunk/stem; sometimes trees and bushes are trained as multiple cordons. The term is also used to describe indeterminate cultivars of tomatoes.

cotyledons (seed leaves) These are the first set of leaves to emerge from the seed case upon germination. In the case of dicotyledons there will be two leaves and in the case of monocotyledons there will be one leaf. These are not the true leaves.

cover crop Very similar to a green manure, this is a temporary crop that is grown on vacant land to protect it from the elements and to smother weed growth.

crop rotation This is carried out to avoid a build up of pests and diseases caused by growing the same crop on the same ground season after season.

crown The main growing point of a perennial plant such as strawberries and sea kale.

cutting A vegetative method of propagating plants using sections of young shoots so that they will be exactly like their parents. The main types used are soft wood, semi-hardwood and hardwood.

damping off A condition caused by fungal diseases such as *Pythium spp.*, *Phytophthora spp.*, *Rhizoctonia solani* and *Botrytis cinerea*, which brings about the collapse and death of young seedlings in trays and pots. It is a problem that is a result of sowing the seeds too thickly, so creating stagnant air conditions around the seedlings, or allowing the compost to become over-wet.

dicotyledons Broad-leaf plants that produce two seed leaves, e.g. bean, tomato.

drill A shallow depression/furrow made in the soil into which seed is sown.

earthing up Drawing soil up around the neck of plants such as potatoes, Brussels sprouts and dwarf French beans.

espalier A branch. Usually used to describe the horizontal tiers or branches of formally trained fruit trees and bushes.

eye An immature growth bud from which shoots will develop; found, for example, on potatoes.

F1 hybrid The first generation of seed that has been collected as the result of a specialized hybrid breeding programme, not to be confused with genetic modification (GM). Seed must not be saved from F1 hybrids because they will not grow true to type.

field capacity soil A soil from which all the drainage water has run off.

foliar feed/spray An application of fertilizer in liquid form that is sprayed all over the leaf surfaces of plants. This is usually carried out during dry weather.

forcing The production of a crop out of its true season, usually by employing greenhouse heating or cloches.

germination The successful emergence of the root and seed leaf from the seed.

grafting A method of propagation used to produce fruit trees. A section of shoot growth is joined to a rootstock.

green manure A short-term crop grown on vacant ground to protect and maintain its fertility and structure.

green waste The organic material that is produced from domestic garden waste by local authorities as part of their recycling programmes. It can be used as a substitute for homemade compost or farmyard manure. It is not suitable for making home seed and potting composts.

hardening off The process of gradually acclimatizing seedlings and plants to the outside growing conditions before planting out.

haulm A term used to describe the foliage of potatoes and peas.

heeling in The practice of providing temporary storage quarters for plants before they are required for planting out. A shallow trench or hole just deep enough to cover the roots of the plants is dug out, then the plants are laid in this at a shallow angle and the roots completely covered with soil. They can remain in this condition for up to four months.

herbicide An industrially produced chemical that is used to kill plants. It can be applied either to the foliage of plants or to the soil/hard surface. Herbicides can be liquid or granular.

humus This is the organic matter content of soil formed by the action of beneficial bacteria on plant material. It continues to decompose in the soil and so it has to be replaced regularly.

intercropping The growing of a quick-maturing crop in between longer-maturing crops, e.g. lettuces between rows of cabbages.

lateral The shoot or stem that grows out of an axil.

leaching The dilution and eventual loss of soluble nutrients or herbicides out of the soil into surrounding watercourses and drains. Leaching could lead to the serious contamination of streams, rivers and other waterways.

leaf mould The fine crumbly organic material that is formed from the decomposed leaves of deciduous trees.

leader The main central shoot on a fruit tree or bush. Sometimes there can be multiple leaders present and these have to be reduced to one.

legume Members of the pea and beans family. They have the ability to form nitrogen-fixing nodules on their roots. These can be of great benefit to the crops that follow.

main crop A crop that is grown to provide the heaviest yields and that can be harvested and put into store for later use, e.g. beetroot, carrots, potatoes.

monocotyledons Narrow-leafed plants that produce a single seed leaf, e.g. onion, rye grass.

mulch A layer of mineral or organic material that is spread over the surface of the soil to conserve moisture and improve the soil structure.

neutral soil A soil that has a pH of 7.

nitrogen (N) The main growth or leaf-forming nutrient.

organic fertilizer Any form of nutrient that is derived from plants (e.g. comfrey) or animals (e.g. bone meal).

organic matter Matter formed from the dead and decaying remains of plants and animals. Also applies to farmyard manure and garden compost.

pan A hard impervious layer of soil under the surface of the soil, usually formed as a result of the persistent use of garden machinery such as rotovators.

perennial A plant whose root system survives for several years, but the top growth dies down each season, e.g. Jerusalem artichoke, asparagus.

permanent wilting point The point at which no more water can be extracted from the soil by the plant, which leads to it wilting permanently.

pesticide Any chemical that is used to kill insects.

pH scale A scale from 0 to 14 used to measure the acidity or alkalinity of soil.

phosphate (P) The main fertilizer to encourage the development of a good root system. Usually applied as superphosphate.

potassium (K) (potash) The main flower- and fruit-forming nutrient.

potting on The moving of a plant established in one size of pot into a pot of the next size up.

predator In biological control terms this is a species that is deliberately introduced into the greenhouse as part of a pest-control programme, e.g. *Encarsia formosa* to control whitefly. In the open garden it refers to insects such as lace wings and ladybirds.

prey Insect pests such as aphids that are controlled by the use of predators (see above).

pricking out The removal of seedlings from a pot or seed tray and either replanting them singly in a flowerpot or spacing them out evenly in plant boxes to grow on to make larger plants before planting them out in the soil.

residual herbicide A herbicide that remains active in the surface of the soil for several months. It forms a toxic layer and kills the young weed seedling as they germinate. Usually used on paths and uncropped areas. They can still cause damage to crop plants for many years after they have been used.

root crop A plant that develops below the surface of the soil, e.g. potato, carrot, parsnip.

rootstock The root system that is used to graft or bud named fruiting varieties on to.

runner A shoot that grows across the surface of the soil. Along the runner small plants are formed that root into the soil, e.g. strawberry.

scion A cutting or shoot containing fruit buds that is taken from one plant, e.g. apple 'Bramley', and is grafted onto a rootstock.

seed leaves The first leaves that appear above the surface of the soil or compost, e.g. the smooth lance-shaped leaves on tomato plants. They should not be mistaken for true leaves.

set Usually describes seed potatoes or immature onion bulbs.

side shoot A shoot or young branch that grows from the axil of a plant such as a tomato.

soil structure Describes the way in which individual soil particles are arranged in groups to form crumbs or clods.

spit The length of the blade of a digging spade: 30 cm (12 inches).

standard A term used to describe a particular type of fruit tree. It has a bare trunk that is 1.8 m (6 ft) long to the point where the uppermost branches are allowed to develop.

string A cluster of fruit that is produced on a single stalk, e.g. cherries, red currants.

subsoil Lies beneath the topsoil and is the intermediate stage in the formation of soil from the parent rock below it.

succession sowing/cropping When several sowings are carried out at different times to allow a crop to be harvested all through the season, maintaining a regular supply and avoiding any gluts or famines, e.g. lettuce.

sulphur Used to reduce the pH level of soils. It can also be used as a fungicide to control mildew, but care must taken when using it because not all plants are tolerant of sulphur.

systemic Describes a herbicide or pesticide that is absorbed into a plant's sap system.

temporary wilting point During hot dry days, plants will appear to wilt because the rate at which the plant loses moisture is greater than it can extract it from the soil. The plants will recover overnight or under cooler conditions.

thinning The removal or reduction of overcrowded seedlings to allow the remaining seedlings to grow on to maturity without any competition.

transplant The moving and planting of a plant to its final growing position, e.g. tomato, cabbage.

tilth Describes the fine, crumbly texture of the surface of the soil, achieved by treading and raking.

tine One of the pointed teeth of a garden fork or rake.

top dressing An application of fertilizer to an actively growing plant.

topsoil The depth to which a soil is cultivated.

true leaves These are leaves that are typical of the plant, e.g. a tomato's true leaves have a ruffled edge.

truss A shoot that carries a cluster of flowers, e.g. on tomato plants.

tuber A compressed stem that resembles a bulb, e.g. potatoes, Jerusalem artichokes.

union The exact point at which the scion has been grafted to the rootstock. It can be seen as a swelling on the trunk about 30 cm (12 inches) above soil level.

water table This is the depth below the surface of the soil at which the soil is waterlogged or saturated.

taking it further

Useful contacts

Seeds

Chiltern Seeds
Bortree Stile
Ulverston
Cumbria
LA12 7PB
Tel: 01229 581 137
Fax: 01229 584 549
Email: info@chilternseeds.co.uk
www.chilternseeds.co.uk

Edwin Tucker and Sons
Brewery Meadow
Stonepark
Ashburton
Devon
TQ13 7DG
Tel: 01364 652233
Fax: 01364 654211
Email: seeds@edwintucker.com
www.edwintucker.com

Kings Seeds and Suffolk Herbs
Monks Farm
Coggeshall Road
Kelvedon
Colchester
Essex
CO5 9PG
Tel: 01376 570000
Fax: 01376 571189
Email: sales@kingsseeds.com
www.kingsseeds.com
www.suffolkherbs.com

Heritage Seed Library
Garden Organic
Ryton Organic Garden
Coventry
CV8 3LG
Tel: 02476 308 232
Fax: 02476 639 229
Email: hsl@gardenorganic.org.uk

Plants of Distinction
Abacus House
Station Yard
Needham Market
Suffolk
IP6 8AS
Tel: 01449 721 720
Orders: 0870 400 9445 Quote POD
Fax: 01449 721 722
Email: sales@plantsofdistinction.co.uk
www.plantsofdistinction.co.uk

Simpson Seeds
The Walled Garden Nursery
Horningsham
Warminster
Wiltshire
BA 12 7NQ
Tel: 01985 845 004
Fax: 01985 845 052
Email: sales@simpsonsseeds.co.uk
www.simpsonsseeds.co.uk

The Real Seed Catalogue
Brithdir Mawr Farm
Newport
Pembrokeshire
SA42 0QJ
Tel: 01239 821 107
Email: info@realseeds.co.uk
www.realseeds.co.uk

Tamar Organics
Cartha Martha Farm
Rezare
Launceston
Cornwall
PL15 9NX
Tel/Fax: 01579 371 087
Email: sales@tamarorganics.co.uk
www.tamarorganics.co.uk

The Organic Catalogue
Riverdene
Molesey Road
Hersham
Surrey
KT12 4RG
Tel: 0845 130 1304
Fax: 01932 252 707
Email: enquiries@chaseorganics.co.uk
www.organiccatalogue.com

Seeds of Italy
C3 Phoenix Industrial Estate
Rosslyn Crescent
Harrow
Middlesex
HA1 2SP
Tel: 0208 427 5020
Fax: 0208 427 5051
Email: grow@italianingredients.com
www.seedsofitaly.com

In the USA

Seeds Trust
PO BOX 596
Cornville
AZ 86325
Tel: (928) 649-3315
Fax: (928) 649-8181
Email: support3@seedstrust.com
www.seedstrust.com

Seeds for the South
Vegetable Seed Warehouse
410 Whaley Pond Road
Graniteville
SC 29829
Email: orders@vegetableseedwarehouse.com
www.seedsforthesouth.com

Fruit trees and bush suppliers

East of England Apples and Orchards
The School House
Rougham
King's Lynn
Norfolk
PE32 2SE
Tel: 01328 838 403
Email: treesales@applesandorchards.org.uk
www.applesandorchards.org.uk
Top fruit; historic cultivars from East Anglia.

Keepers Nursery
Gallants Court
Gallants Lane
East Farleigh
Maidstone
Kent
ME15 0LE
Tel: 01622 726 465
Fax: 0870 705 2145
Email: info@keepers-nursery.co.uk
www.keepers-nursery.co.uk
Top and soft fruit; probably the best nursery in the country.

Reads Nursery
Hales Hall
Loddon
Norfolk
NR14 6QW
Tel: 01508 548 395
Fax: 01508 548 040
Email: sales@readsnursery.co.uk
www.readsnursery.co.uk
Top and soft fruit; national collections of figs and citrus.

Rogers of Pickering
The Nurseries
Malton Road
Pickering
North Yorkshire
YO18 7JW
Tel: 01751 472 226
www.rvroger.co.uk
Top and soft fruit; excellent gooseberry selection.

Walcot Organic Nursery
Lower Walcot Farm
Walcot Lane
Drakes Broughton
Pershore
Worcestershire
WR10 2AL
Tel/Fax: 01905 841 587
Email: enquiries@walcotnursery.co.uk
www.walcotnursery.co.uk
Top fruit; specializing in organic fruit trees and rootstocks. Soil
Association Certificated.

Welsh Fruit Stocks
Bryngwyn
Kington
Hereford
HR5 3QZ
Tel/Fax: 01497 851 209
Email: sian@welshfruitstocks.co.uk
www.welshfruitstocks.co.uk
Organic soft fruit. First-class selection.

Agroforestry
46 Hunters Moon
Dartington
Totnes
Devon
TQ9 6JT
Tel/Fax: 01803 840 776
Email: mail@agroforestry.co.uk
www.agroforestry.co.uk
Top and soft fruit specialists and sundries.

Ken Muir
Rectory Road
Weeley Heath
Clacton-on-Sea
Essex
CO16 9BJ
Tel: 0870 747 9111 and 01255 830 181
Fax: 01255 831 534
Email: info@kenmuir.co.uk
www.kenmuir.co.uk
Top and soft fruit.

Thornhayes Nursery
St Andrews Wood
Dulford
Cullompton
Devon
EX15 2DF
Tel: 01884 266 746
Fax: 01884 266 739
Email: trees@thornhayes-nursery.co.uk
www.thornhayes-nursery.co.uk
Top and soft fruit.

Scott's Nurseries
4 Higher Street
Merriott
Somerset
TA16 5PL
Tel: 01460 723 06
Fax: 01460 774 33
Email: sales@scottsnurseries.co.uk
www.scottsnurseries.co.uk
Top and soft fruit.

In the USA
Trees of Antiquity
20 Wellsona Road
Paso Robles
CA 93446
Tel: (805) 467-9909
Fax: (805) 467-9909
www.treesofantiquity.com

Raintree Nursery
391 Butts Road Morton
WA 98356
Tel: (360) 496-6400
Fax: 1 (888) 770-8358
Email: customerservice@raintreenursey.com
www.raintreenursery.com

Fruit cages, netting products and garden sundries

Haxnicks Ltd
Beaumont Business Centre
Woodlands Road
Mere
Wiltshire
BA12 6BT
Tel: 0845 241 1555
Fax: 0845 241 1550
Email: sales@haxnicks.co.uk
www.haxnicks.co.uk
Netting and other plant protection products.

Harrod Horticultural
Pinbush Road
Lowestoft
Suffolk
NR33 7NL
Tel: 0845 402 5300 (sales)
Fax: 01502 582 456
Email: enquiries@harrod.uk.com
www.harrodhorticultural.com
Fruit cage netting and raised bed kits.

In the USA
The Garden Shop at Lakewold Gardens
12317 Gravelly Lake Drive SW
Lakewood
WA 98499
Tel: (252) 224-2300
www.gardenshoponline.com

Greenhouses and greenhouse equipment

Two Wests and Elliott
Unit 4 Carrwood Road
Sheepbridge Industrial Estate
Chesterfield
Derbyshire
S41 9RH
Tel: 01246 451 077
Fax: 01246 260 115
www.twowests.co.uk

CLM Keder Greenhouses Ltd
Newtown
Offenham
Evesham
Worcestershire
WR11 8RZ
Tel: 01386 490 94
Fax: 01386 421 605
Email: sales@kedergreenhouse.co.uk
www.kedergreenhouse.co.uk
Innovative greenhouse specialists.

In the USA
EnviroCept
8 West Sunrise
Benton City
WA 99320
Tel: 1 (888) 326-8634
Fax: (509) 271-4471
www.envirocept.com

Juliana Greenhouses
2385 Goodhue Street
Red Wing
MN 55066
Tel: (800) 681-3302
www.julianagreenhouses.com

Spades, forks and other garden tools

Bulldog Tools
Clarington Forge
Wigan
Lancashire
Tel: 01279 401 572
www.bulldogtools.co.uk

Fiskars
Fiskars Brands UK Ltd
Newlands Avenue
Bridgend
CF31 2XA
Tel: 01656 655 595
Fax: 01656 659 582
Email: enquiries@fiskars.co.uk
www.fiskarsgarden.co.uk

Wolf Garden Ltd
Unit 2
The Triangle
Wildwood Drive
Worcester
WR5 2QX
Tel: 01905 353 308
Fax: 01905 354 416
Email: info@uk.wolf-garten.com
www.wolf-garten.co.uk
Manufacturers of snap-on tools.

In the USA
Ames True Temper
465 Railroad Avenue
Camp Hill
PA 17001-8859
Tel: 1 (800) 393-1846
Fax: (717) 730-2552
www.ames.com

Barnel USA
4888 NW Bethany Blvd
Suite K5-375
Portland
Oregon 97229-9260
Tel: 1 (800) 877-9907
Email: info@barnel.com
www.barnel.com

Growing medium
Fertile Fibre
Withington Court
Withington
Herefordshire
HR1 3RJ
Tel: 01432 853 111
Fax: 01432 850 191
Email: sales@fertilefibre.co.uk
www.fertilefibre.co.uk
Coir-based composts and other non-peat products.

Melcourt Industries Ltd
Boldridge Brake
Long Newnton
Tetbury
Gloucestershire
GL8 8RT
Tel: 01666 502 711
Fax: 01666 504 398
Email: mail@melcourt.co.uk
www.melcourt.co.uk
Potting composts, bark and other growing media.

Biological and other pest controls

Scarletts Plantcare
Nayland Road
West Bergholt
Colchester
CO6 3DH
Tel: 01206 240 466
Fax: 01206 242 530
Email: info@scarletts.co.uk
www.scarletts.co.uk

Nemasys
Customer services
Becker Underwood Ltd
Harwood Industrial Estate
Harwood Road
Littlehampton
West Sussex
BN17 7AU
Tel: 01252 408 820
Email: info.uk@beckerunderwood.com
www.nemasysinfo.com
All forms of biological pest control.

Aston Horticulture
PO Box 183
Cranleigh
Surrey
GU6 9AH
Tel: 0870 350 6250
Fax: 0870 350 6251
Email: sales@astonhorticulture.com
www.astonhorticulture.com
Garlic-based plant protection.

Societies and organizations

National Society of Allotment and Leisure Gardeners – NSALG
O'Dell House
Hunters Road
Corby
Northamptonshire
NN17 5JE
Tel: 01536 266 576
Fax: 01536 264 509
Email: natsoc@nsalg.org.uk
www.nsalg.org.uk

Royal Horticultural Society
RHS Garden Wisley
Woking
Surrey
GU23 6QB
Tel: 0845 260 9000
www.rhs.org.uk
Membership and administration
Tel: 0845 062 1111 (UK)
The UK's leading gardening charity.

Garden Organic
Ryton Organic Gardens
Ryton
Coventry
CV8 3LG
Tel: 02476 303 517
Fax: 02476 639 229
Email: enquiry@gardenorganic.org.uk
www.gardenorganic.org.uk
Europe's leading organic gardening charity; the home of the Heritage Seed Library.

Soil Association
South Plaza
Marlborough Street
Bristol
BS1 3NX
Tel: 0117 314 5000
Fax: 0117 314 5001
Email: sass@soilassociation.org
www.soilassociation.org

Brogdale Horticultural Trust
Brogdale Farm
Brogdale Road
Faversham
Kent
ME13 8XZ
Tel: 01795 535 286
Email: info@brogdale.org
www.brogdale.org
Holders of the National Fruit Collection.

English Heritage
Customer Services
PO Box 569
Swindon
Wiltshire
SN2 2YP
Tel: 0870 333 1181
Fax: 01793 414 926
Email: customers@english-hertiage.org.uk
www.english-heritage.org.uk

National Trust
The National Trust
PO Box 39
Warrington
WA5 7WD
Tel: 0844 800 1895; Minicom: 0844 800 4410
Fax: 0844 800 4642
Email: enquiries@thenationaltrust.org.uk
www.nationaltrust.org.uk

National Vegetable Society
5 Whitelow Road
Heaton Moor
Stockport
SK4 4BY
Tel: 0161 442 7190
www.nvsuk.org.uk

Which? Gardening
2 Marylebone Road
London
NW1 4DF
Email: gardening@which.co.uk
www.which.co.uk/gardening
Independent consumer reports and expert advice.

National Council for the Conservation of Plants and Gardens – NCCPG
12 Home Farm
Loseley Park
Guildford
GU3 1HS
Tel: 01483 447 540
Fax: 01483 458 933
Email: info@nccpg.org.uk
www.nccpg.com

Further reading

Books

Alcott, Louisa May and Harper, Kate (2008) *Royal Horticultural Society Vegetable and Fruit Gardening*, London: Dorling Kindersley.

Baker, Henry (1998) *The Fruit Garden Displayed*, London: Cassell Illustrated.

Bird, Richard (2006) *Pruning Fruiting Plants*, London: Southwater.

Foster, Clare (2007) *Your Allotment*, London: Cassell Illustrated.

Garden Organic (2008) *Encyclopedia of Organic Gardening*, London: Dorling Kindersley.

Hamilton, Geoff (2008) *Organic Gardening*, London: Dorling Kindersley.

Hessayon, Dr D. G. (1990) *The Fruit Expert*, Walthom Cross: PBI Publications.

Hessayon, Dr D. G. (1997) *The Vegetable and Herb Expert*, Walthom Cross: PBI Publications.

Larkcom, Joy (2007) *Oriental Vegetables*, London: Frances Lincoln.

Pikington, George (2005) *Composting with Worms*, Bath: Eco-Logic Books.

Magazines

Garden News
Grow it!
Grow Your Own
Kitchen Garden
Organic Gardening

conversion tables

The nearest approximate equivalent for both the metric and imperial systems.

Temperature conversions

Celsius	Fahrenheit
0	32
5	42
10	50
15	58
20	68
25	78
30	92
35	97
38	100

Measurement conversions

Metric	Imperial
3 mm	$\frac{1}{8}$ inch
6 mm	¼ (0.25) inch
12.5 mm	½ (0.5) inch
18 mm	¾ (0.75) inch
25 mm	1 inch
30 cm	1 ft
91.4 cm	3 ft (1 yard)
1 m	39.9 inches
0 .836 m^2	1 yard^2
1 m^2	1.9 yard^2
1 hectare	2.4 acres

Weight conversions

Solids

Grams	Pounds and ounces
30 g	1 oz
120 g	4 oz (¼ lb)
240 g	8 oz (½ lb)
450 g	16 oz (1 lb)
1000 g	2.2 lb
50 kg	1 cwt

Liquids

1000 millilitres = 1 litre

8 pints = 1 gallon

Millilitres	Pints
70 ml	$\frac{1}{8}$ pint
145 ml	¼ pint
280 ml	½ pint
568 ml	1 pint
1 litre	1¾ pints
4.5 litres	1 gallon

index